NOSTALGIC
HULL

The publishers would like to thank the following companies for their

support in the production of this book

Arco Ltd

N R Burnett Ltd

De Smet Rosedowns Ltd

Donaldson Fiter Components Ltd

EYMS Group Ltd

Fenner Plc

Henry Hird Ltd

Hull Fish Auction Ltd

Hull Truck Theatre

Humber Electrical Engineering Co. Ltd

Ideal Standard

Wm Jackson & Son Ltd

K Comm Group

Reckitt Benckiser

Robinson & Sawdon Ltd

Sandhill Garden Centre

F R Scott

G F Smith & Sons

First published in Great Britain by True North Books Limited
Britannia Works, Halifax, England. HX3 6AE
01422 344344

ISBN 978-1906649012

Text, design and origination by True North Books
Printed and bound by The Amadeus Press

NOSTALGIC
HULL

CONTENTS

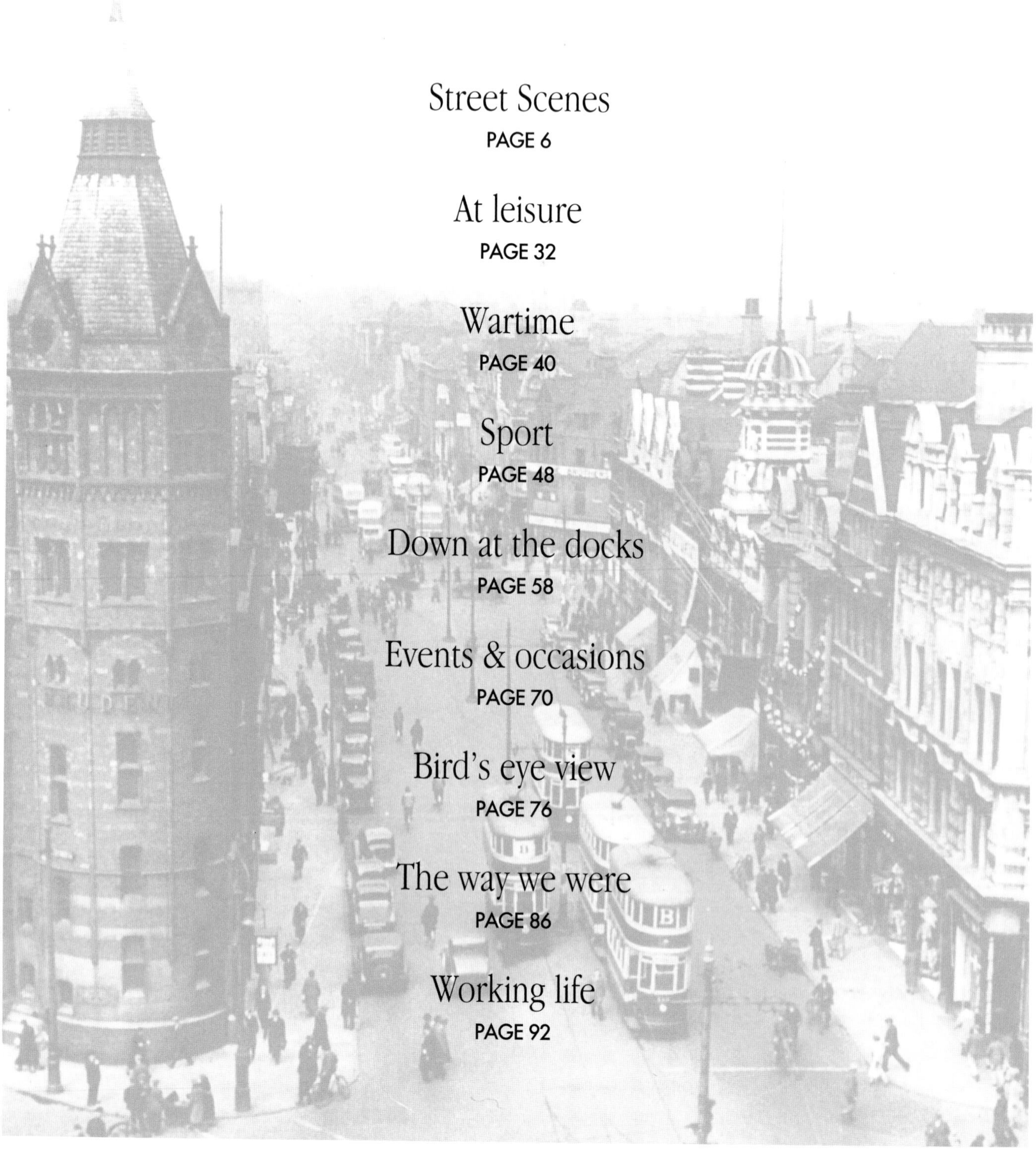

Street Scenes

PAGE 6

At leisure

PAGE 32

Wartime

PAGE 40

Sport

PAGE 48

Down at the docks

PAGE 58

Events & occasions

PAGE 70

Bird's eye view

PAGE 76

The way we were

PAGE 86

Working life

PAGE 92

INTRODUCTION

As the 20th century disappears into the mists of time, there becomes a moment when certain events and customs of that era begin to take on a new role. The more recent years of the last quarter of that century are still relatively fresh, but before then lie decades that are starting to take on the mantle of 'the good old days'. For younger readers, even the swinging 60s belong to their childhood and, for the younger still, the hippy culture is part of their parents' folklore. It is now getting on for 40 years since we stopped having shillings and pence in our purses and talked of holidays abroad as something of an adventure. So, with that in mind, welcome to 'Nostalgic Hull', a book that will whisk you back to the days when boys' hair was as long as that of their girlfriends and then beyond those times to the earlier days of the last century. It was a fabulous period of great change and much of that is reflected in the wonderful images and pithy captions that accompany them. The 1900s began with an old monarch on the throne as Britain ruled the waves and huger tracts of the world map were coloured red. Steam and horse power provided much of the energy we needed to get ourselves and our chattels around and coal fired our industries and heated our homes. Within a few years, motor cars appeared on the streets, electric trams rattled along at their side and man took to the air in flimsy machines that seemed to defy all the natural laws as they somehow stayed aloft. The world stage was also in flux and great nations soon faced one another across trenches in one of the most costly conflicts known to mankind as millions died in the cockpit of Europe.

'Nostalgic Hull' takes us on a trip down memory lane to when flat caps were de rigueur for all working men and women wore dresses with hems that dragged along the floor. After that, we come to the Depression years and difficult times in the interwar period as our major industries fell into recession and families struggled on or below the breadline. The book charts the course through the war with Hitler and into the austerity period that followed, before the recovery of late 1950s and 1960s. But change was always with us, and we suffered the draught as traditional industries at the dockside felt the pinch and the new world of technology and communications became the main force, sweeping away the old and bringing in the modern ways like some form of Aladdin and his new lamp. However, even this pantomime character realised that his old one was the better model, so not everything that altered was for the best. Morals, standards of behaviour and attitudes towards weaker brethren were called into question as the final quarter of the last century got under way. It is not for the authors of this book to pass judgement, but they can offer the images of the ways in which our city once looked and its citizens formerly conducted themselves for readers to draw their own conclusions.

This is not a dry and dusty history book, but one that focuses on the nostalgia that we have for days gone by through which we, our mums and dads and their parents lived. We can read elsewhere about how Wyke upon Hull came into being in medieval times and of the visits of King Edward I in the 14th century when a licence was granted to build fortifications at 'Kyngeston-super-Hill' (the King's town upon Hull). Now is the moment to recreate the scenes when the washing machine was a luxury and donkey stoning the front step was a work of art. This book will help you remember the taste of ginger beer and dandelion and burdock. Wind up record players scratched out melodies grooved on old 78s as we tapped our feet to the sounds of the big bands of Tommy Dorsey and Paul Whiteman or swooned at Sinatra, Johnny Ray and Guy Mitchell. In those days we had pubs that sold ale you could taste and we played games of don, cribbage and dominoes' fives and threes. Turn off the digital TV and settle back in your favourite chair. It is time to think of Toni perms, trams and trolley buses or purchasing bullseyes by the ounce and not the gram. Last, but by no means least we would like to thank the numerous prominent Hull companies who have supported the production of this book. Within these pages the story of each of them is told - their own proud histories and prospects for the future adding to the rich tapestry of life in Hull. Let the nostalgic journey begin...

TEXT	ANDREW MITCHELL, STEVE AINSWORTH
PHOTOGRAPH COMPILATION	TONY LAX
DESIGNER	SEAMUS MOLLOY
BUSINESS DEVELOPMENT EDITOR	PETER PREST

STREET SCENES

The photographer was positioned close to where the Castle Street and Garrison Road intersection of the A63 now stands, heavy with traffic heading out across Myton Bridge and toward Hessle Road and Clive Sullivan Way to access the M62. Such noise and speed associated with modern vehicles was unheard of to people living in late Victorian times. The view along Market Place from Queen Street shows just how important the horse was at the start of the 20th century. The pony and trap or horse and carriage was the way to get about for those with a few bob in their pockets as they either owned such a mode of transport or could afford a taxi ride in one. Ordinary folk relied on the horse tramway that flourished in the final quarter of the 19th century before being withdrawn in 1899. After a brief flirtation with steam powered trams, Hull went over to electrification of the system, with the first route being inaugurated on 5 July, 1899, along Anlaby Road and Hessle Road. 'King Billy' has continued to ride his steed, impervious to all the changes, just as he first did in 1734 when the statue was erected. 'Our great deliverer', as his plinth puts it, was restored to its former glory 20 years ago when tarnishing and grime was removed.

Right: This site was once the largest dock in the UK. It measured 518 metres long and 75 metres wide. Queen's Dock opened in 1778 and was known as 'the dock' until the opening of the Humber Dock, when the word 'old' was added to its description. Renamed formally in 1854, it continued in existence until 1930 when it was filled in and, later, turned into pleasure gardens. As the dock was not fully filled in, Queen's Gardens are largely below the level of the surrounding streets. The photograph was taken in the early days of the gardens' existence and there is now a line of trees down the central avenue that leads to the Wilberforce Monument. The dramatic impact of this homage to the great abolitionist has been lessened since the early 1960s when Hull College was built behind it. William Wilberforce (1759-1833) became the town's Member of Parliament at the tender age of 21 and worked tirelessly as a reformer, being a fervent believer that the slave trade was barbarous and evil. His monument was erected at the end of Whitefriargate in 1835, where it stood for a century before being regarded as a major hazard for motorists. It was moved to Queen's Gardens in 1935 in a ceremony attended by Mrs Arnold Reckitt, Wilberforce's great granddaughter. The gardens were officially opened by Herbert Morrison, deputy leader of the Labour Party.

Below: It was at the start of the swinging 60s when cars were parked bumper to bumper at the top of Alfred Gelder Street, close to the statue of Charles Henry Wilson (1833-1907). The Wilson shipping line was, at one time, the largest privately owned fleet in the world. The Wilson family members were leading lights in the business and social life of the city in Victorian and Edwardian times. Charles Wilson served as the High Sheriff of Hull and in 1874 was elected as a Member of Parliament. Although opposed to the Boer War, he lent the company's best vessel, the 'Ariosto', to the war effort. He was married to Jane Wellesley, a great niece of the Duke of Wellington. In 1906, he was raised to the peerage as Baron Nunburnholme. Alfred Gelder Street was created in 1901 as part of a programme of street development that largely helped create the current pattern of traffic routes. It was named in honour of William Alfred Gelder (1854-1941), co-founder of Gelder and Kitchen, architects of some renown. He became Hull's Mayor in 1899, a post he held five times in all, and was a major figure in the redevelopment of the city centre and the building of Drypool Bridge. He was knighted in 1903.

Left: Holy Trinity Church, observed in this late Victorian photograph, is an architectural oasis situated in the middle of some less than elegant buildings in between King Street and Market Place. Here, we are looking at the west end of the church that was established in about 1285 and is one of the largest parish churches in England. It was set up as a chapel of ease to Hessle, but was not consecrated until 1425 and did not achieve parish status until 1661. The oldest sections can be found in the brick transepts. Restoration was begun by HF Lockwood in 1841 and further work took place during the period of 1859 to 1872. This latter work was under the guidance of the eminent George Gilbert Scott. He was responsible for a large portfolio of impressive projects that included St Mary's Cathedral, Glasgow, Christchurch Cathedral, New Zealand, London's Albert Memorial and Leeds General Infirmary. FS Brodrick undertook some more work on the church in 1906. A statue to the poet Andrew Marvell stands close by. The dates on this memorial show his life dates 1620-70, but other historians believe them to be 1621-78. His father was the lecturer at Holy Trinity and Andrew was a pupil at Hull Grammar School.

Left: Old streets in Hull's 'Old Town' include Silver Street, Manor Street, Posterngate, Black Friar Gate, High Street and the Market Place. High Street, pictured here in 1905, was once the most important street in the whole city and is the home to Wilberforce House, the birthplace of the anti-slavery campaigner William Wilberforce (1759-1833). Wilberforce House is now a museum dedicated to the history of the slave trade. Wilberforce was elected as a Member of Parliament at the age of twenty-one and later became known as 'The Nightingale of the House of Commons' because of his campaigning work. Wilberforce was the leading figure in the campaign to abolish the slave trade and his work resulted in The Abolition Act of 1833 which abolished slavery throughout the British Empire.

Right: What an idyllic scene of Eastgate, Hessle, captured for posterity by the cameraman in the early Spring of 1910. The picture could almost have been posed for the occasion, but in reality the cameraman was just very lucky. Almost like a film set everything is here: boys wearing Eton collars, girls in smocks and ladies in long Edwardian dresses. These were the days when playing out meant playing in the middle of the street. Right at the end of the road is a gas lamp, the focus of so many memories in every street. On dark nights the single lamp was focus for childhood gatherings. Bigger, braver boys would climb it and open its glass sides to see how it worked. With a rope attached it could be a swing; in the summer it was the stumps for a game of street cricket.

Right: This rather Heath Robinson affair was photographed in June, 1936. As a feature of the history of renewable energy, it has some significance as it probably dates from Victorian times. Used as a wind pump, it helped dispense water from a flat area as an agricultural and irrigation aid for surrounding fields. In appearance, it has more in common with Don Quixote and his jousting escapades than it does with the modern sails that we see swirling across the tops of some of our hills in modern times. They have become something of a controversial issue. Greens would have you believe that they can provide a real alternative to the burning of fossil fuels or the reliance on nuclear power as we attempt to find better ways of creating energy for our homes and industries. Reactionaries deplore the noise of the whirling arms and the unsightly blot they make upon our countryside. They also believe that the amount of energy that can be harnessed from 21st century windmills is a pitiful fraction of what would be needed to make them economically and environmentally effective.

'**M**onument Bridge' - actually the Whitefriargate Lock bridge, occupied this site until 1932. The 'Monument' on the left is the Wilberforce Monument, erected in 1834 (and which was later relocated to Wilberforce Drive in front of Hull College). This busy scene was captured in the early 1900s and is surely a perfect example of Edwardian Hull. On the far left at the base of the Monument a lady is wearing an unmistakeable example of the hats of the period. No motor vehicles are in sight but the tram is evidence that the white-hot heat of technology is changing the world. For the time being however, both shanks pony and real ponies continue to predominate.

Above: Queen Victoria was still on the throne, just, when this photo was taken of the trams travelling along Hull's King Edward Street. No doubt many younger folk imagine that the street was named after Queen Victoria's son who only came to the throne s Edward VII a year after this picture was taken. The monarch in question is of course a much older King Edward. It was in 1293 that King Edward I 'the Hammer of the Scots' bought the port to use as a supply base for his military campaigns in Scotland. In 1299, the king founded the borough of 'Kings town' or Kingston-upon-Hull on the site, and still the formal title of our city.

Below: Here is 'Monument Bridge' pictured in the early 1930s before it disappeared for good. The City Centre Pedestrianisation Scheme eventually saw the diversion of the west end of Alfred Gelder Street into Queen's Dock Avenue and the creation of a bus lane over 'Monument Bridge' - a name really referring to the Whitefriargate Lock bridge, which occupied the site between 1829 and 1932. The 'Monument' was the Wilberforce Monument, which was originally erected nearby in 1834 (and which was later relocated to Wilberforce Drive in front of Hull College). During the course of the pedestrianisation works, parts of the substructure of the last bridge (built in 1905) were exposed and three of its T-shaped piers subsequently put on public display opposite the remains of the Beverley Gate at the west end of Whitefriargate.

Above: Pictured here in 1903, Market Place, Hull looks decidedly quiet. It was not always so. In 1279 Hull was granted the right to hold a market and a fair. People would come from all over Northeast England to buy and sell goods in the town. Early markets and fairs could be riotous events, with not only swarms of stallholders but lots of entertainment such as dog fights, bear and bull baiting - not to mention gambling and excessive drinking. By the Edwardian era such bad behaviour was far in the past. In the market-place stands a fine equestrian statue of King William III. On the pedestal is this inscription:- "This statue was erected in 1734, to the memory of King William, our great deliverer." As William of Orange he had 'saved' Britain from Catholicism and the return of the Stewarts.

Right: Here's a sight seldom seen: elephants trooping through the narrow streets pf Beverley. The date is the close of the 19th century; the occasion is a visit to the town by Barnum and Bailey's American circus. Barnum & Bailey's tour of Great Britain in 1898 was organised like a huge military operation. The circus swept through the country, staying only one or two days at each location. No sooner was the show over than the whole operation was on the move again - the tents were pulled down whilst the artistes ate their supper. It was not simply a matter of moving over eight hundred people and the circus equipment - the travelling menagerie was larger than anything seen in Britain before or since. Travelling as part of the show were four hundred horses, twenty elephants, camels, zebras, lions, and Johanna the famous Giant Gorilla. The whole enterprise travelled by road to the nearest railway goods yard to be taken by train to the next booking.

Above: This undated photograph records life as it was once lived in Manchester Place off Waverley Street. Though the flagstones are clearly swept clean and the residents took pride in their homes the heart now sinks to imagine what it was like to be brought up in such a dark, dim canyon. Yet for thousands of folk crammed into tiny houses thrown up at the height of Hull's glory days such homes, without benefit of bathrooms and gardens, were the norm. Yet many folk who knew these streets would say that living in such close nit communities was far superior to life in modern blocks of flats where few people know their neighbours.

Below: People were scurrying like ants in this photograph from the 1930s that was taken at the height of the depression years that saw unemployment in Britain top 3 million. Shipbuilding and associated dock work went into a major decline and families that relied on the sea, in one way or another, for their livelihood found it hard to make ends meet. At times, neighbours fought with neighbours as they shoved one another aside when workers were being taken on for a day's shift on the quayside. More often than not there was nothing to be had and men sat around with an empty expression on their faces and even emptier bellies. Being the breadwinner was hard enough, but having to go home and face a wife who could not manage to feed the children properly was hard, very hard. For some, there was no such problem. Those in white collar jobs seemed to manage and, all the while, the gap between the haves and have nots widened. In Queen Victoria Square, there were plenty of people going about their business or popping into the shops. It was a different story in the disadvantaged parts of the city.

Right: In the late 1920s when Jameson Street was photographed it was thronged with shoppers wandering across the road. Both trams and cars were few and slow; the danger of being run over was slight, and shoppers still used to the speed of horse and cart gave little thought to what the future might hold. Those that did think of the future were more likely to predict one of fewer rather than more motorcars. The 1920s was a prosperous decade a this scene testifies; the 1930s which followed however, saw one of the worst economic depressions in history, one which brought unprecedented poverty and unemployment in its wake.

Below: 'Plenty of Pure Gelatine' says the sign in the window of Norman Johnstones' grocer's shop in Hessle. It's hard to imagine that a similar sign today would result in queues like this. In fact it is unlikely that gelatine alone was the cause of this long line of folk - or indeed anything that there was plenty of. The outbreak of the Second World War brought in its wake food rationing as German U-boats took an awesome toll of Britain's merchant navy and the food it carried from abroad. A generation of youngsters brought up during the war had no idea what to do with a banana when getting handed one for the first time after the war's end. Having a ration book and coupons was little use if there was nothing to buy with them. Here it looks as if word has got round of some fresh supplies having been recently delivered.

Queen Victoria Square is the effective heart of the modern city. It was once known as City Square, but the name of the famous old monarch gives the place a friendlier feel. It is from here that the streets opening onto the commercial and retail parts of the city radiate. But there was a distinct lack of good feeling in the square towards the enemy in the aftermath of the air raid that hit Hull on the night of 7/8 May, 1941. The sirens sounded just before midnight, warning the local population of the impending arrival of bombers that were originally intending to target Liverpool. It is thought that some 72 aircraft were involved in the attack on industrial and dock installations. Over 100 tons of high explosive and nearly 10,000 incendiary bombs were dropped in the devastating assault. Major fires raged across the

riverside quays, railway, domestic property and the commercial heartland. Barges tied up in the docks were sunk and RAF pilots returning from a mission on the continent reported seeing Hull on fire as they flew from the Danish coastline and over the North Sea. We lost 264 poor souls that night, with hundreds of others injured. The population responded bravely and every single member of the Civil Defence, male or female, whether on rota or not, reported in to headquarters. Schoolchildren turned out to act as messengers, providing an invaluable service as normal communications had been disrupted. Despite all the carnage around her, Queen Victoria remained aloof on her pedestal, bloodied but unbowed. The statue seemed to embody the spirit of the people. They had been damaged by the attack, but were even more determined than ever that Herr Hitler and his bully boys must not succeed. The same sense of purpose was mirrored across the nation during the period that became known as 'the blitz'. The attacks on our major industrial cities and, later, the historical ones targeted in the 'Baedeker raids', began in earnest in the late summer of 1940 with the attack on London in early September. The targets were soon spread across the country, from Glasgow to Exeter and all points in between. The intensity had slackened by the start of the following summer as the RAF meted out aerial justice to many of the enemy bombing squadrons and Germany's attention turned towards the invasion of Russia. Eventually, Queen Victoria Square would return to its former glory, but it took time to rebuild and life was never quite the same again.

Instead of signs for Guinness and Schweppes, the far side of Paragon Square that connects with Paragon Street is now home to such delights as Naomi's Bar, Café M and a place offering body piercing and tattoo's (sic) with the obligatory misplaced apostrophe that blights many establishments, especially those offering teas. Ferensway is now even busier with traffic than it was in 1962, acting as a link between the roads to Beverley to the right and the Humber Bridge to the left. This section of the A1079 was named for Thomas Robinson Ferens (1847-1930), the former chairman of Reckitt's and local benefactor. He served as a Liberal MP from 1906-18 and gifted land for recreational uses in addition to the funds needed to build the city centre art gallery that bears his name. The figures gazing from the square across Ferensway are of a soldier helping an injured comrade. This sculpture is a memorial to those who fell in the Boer Wars. It was unveiled on 5 November, 1904 and was funded by public subscription. The cenotaph marking those who fell in the Great War stands to its rear. An official ceremony remembering those killed in action was held here in September, 1924.

Above: Though peace in 1945 saw British aviation move increasingly towards civilian aircraft production pictured here at Brough are Blackburn Beverley military transport planes which came into service in 1955. The site at Brough dates back to 1916 when the Blackburn Aeroplane & Motor Company built a new factory there. The company flourished through the war years and the proximity of the River Humber meant the factory was ideally situated for the launching of seaplanes. In the years between the two world wars the company's reputation grew, and in 1939 it became Blackburn Aircraft Ltd. In 1960 the company became the Hawker Blackburn Division of the giant Hawker Siddeley Aviation Combine which in 1965 became simply Hawker Siddeley, Brough, and later part of the British Aerospace Kingston-Brough Division.

Below: Here's the Subway Service Station in Hessle Road pictured as it was some fifty years ago. The modern petrol station began to proliferate in the 1960s, but we tend to forget that petrol stations until then commonly provided petrol directly onto the street. No one seemed to object to the now obvious dangers of storing vast quantities of highly flammable petrol just yards from people's homes. But if we were oblivious to the dangers we were grateful for real service. None of today's self service, back then motorists expected and got their cars filled up without even having to step out of their vehicles. The petrol attendant came out of the garage, asked the driver what he (it was rarely she) wanted and then dispensed change from a leather bag at his waist. No need for service under cover, if it was raining it was the attendant who got wet not the driver.

Right: The elevated panorama across the corner of Queen Victoria Square shows the edge of Princes Dock as it looked in 1953. This was the year of the Queen's Coronation and the start of what we hoped would be a new Elizabethan era. The country was still feeling the effects of the austere postwar years and there was rationing to some extent. This would not completely disappear until the following

year. The new shopping centre and waterside cafes now dominate the place where the ship's rigging can be seen, but Burtons continues to be the 'tailor of taste' on the corner of Whitefriargate, though the building and its lettering have a much more modern look nowadays. In the 1950s, there were several major men's tailors vying for business. John Collier had 'the window to watch' and there were Weaver to Wearer, Hepworth's, Alexandre and the Fifty Shilling Tailor competing hard for trade. Burton has come through many difficult times and has done well to survive as many competitors went to the wall as demand for traditional items, such as jackets, three piece suits and smartly tailored trousers, fell in the swinging 60s and the flower power 70s.

Gelder (1854-1941), co-founder of Gelder and Kitchen, architects of some renown. He became Hull's Mayor in 1899, a post he held five times in all, and was a major figure in the redevelopment of the city centre and the building of Drypool Bridge. He was knighted in 1903.

Below: We blame global warming for all sorts of meteorological events today. The hurricane that flattened New Orleans in 2005, the baking hot summer in Britain of 2006 that was followed by two of downpours and floods, and the disappearance of traditional snowy winters are all the fault of climate change. Yet, we tend to forget that we have had fluctuations in the past. We had a drought in 1976, the big freeze of 1963 that replicated one in 1947 and the major flooding that occurred in 1953, particularly down the East Coast. Not much was said about the greenhouse effect on those occasions. This is a scene from Lairgate, Beverley. In 1953, the River Hull had burst its banks and, although the people posing for the picture seem to be in good spirits, the flooding was depressing for them. The dirty water, containing all sorts of unmentionables, was carried across the thresholds of their homes, rendering carpets unusable and leaving a smelly residue when the water level receded. Furniture was damaged, and all this in an

Above: It was at the start of the swinging 60s when cars were parked bumper to bumper at the top of Alfred Gelder Street, close to the statue of Charles Henry Wilson (1833-1907). The Wilson shipping line was, at one time, the largest privately owned fleet in the world. The Wilson family members were leading lights in the business and social life of the city in Victorian and Edwardian times. Charles Wilson served as the High Sheriff of Hull and in 1874 was elected as a Member of Parliament. Although opposed to the Boer War, he lent the company's best vessel, the 'Ariosto', to the war effort. He was married to Jane Wellesley, a great niece of the Duke of Wellington. In 1906, he was raised to the peerage as Baron Nunburnholme. Alfred Gelder Street was created in 1901 as part of a programme of street development that largely helped create the current pattern of traffic routes. It was named in honour of William Alfred

area where many working class folk could not afford the insurance premiums that would have resulted in financial assistance to tide them over.

Below: The war memorial depicting a soldier helping a colleague in the Boer War evokes memories of the story told by Rolf Harris in his tear jerking 'Two little boys' that topped the singles charts in 1969. In that ditty the Australian entertainer sang of a man risking his own life to rescue a fallen friend. It is such an example of selflessness that the sculptor of the memorial portrayed so successfully. The 27 names on the memorial will never be forgotten, nor will those on the one behind erected after the Great War.

Paragon Station, seen in the 1962 photograph, is no more in this form. The remodelled Interchange has taken its place. The ABC cinema, further along Ferensway, opened on 26 January, 1934, as the Regal. Its vast auditorium contained seating for 2,553 in stalls and a single balcony. A full size stage was located behind the proscenium arch and was used for theatrical and musical productions. It was especially popular as a pop music venue in the 1960s hosting shows by the chart toppers of the era, including Cliff Richard and the Beatles. By then, it had long become the ABC. It was renamed Cannon, but closed on 29 June, 1989. The C and A store opposite, beyond Jameson Street, is now TJ Hughes and Hammonds belongs to the House of Fraser.

Above: Whitefriargate is always thronged with shoppers, but the cars at the kerbside in this 1971 photograph have long been taken out of the equation. Leading now towards the Princes Quay Shopping Centre, the street has its place in the city's history. In the 19th century, this was a very fashionable area. It led out from the old town towards the newly developing suburbs that were springing up beyond the city walls. Parliament Street, which leads away to the right of the camera, has some of the most impressive architecture in the area and is currently home to an array of solicitors and other similar professional businesses. Ahead of the camera, beyond where the Joshua Tetley dray is turning into Princes Dock Street, is a spot close to the site of the Wilberforce Monument that stood there until the mid 1930s. Just nearby, the foundations of Beverly Gate remain as a form of memorial to the time when King Charles I was refused entry to the town. In April 1642, an anti Royalist faction led by the Governor of Hull, Sir John Hotham, closed the gates on the King, thus sowing the seeds of the English Civil War.

Below: The bus sweeping across the Jameson Street/George Street intersection from Prospect Street towards the camera on King Edward Street is now a manoeuvre that can be committed to the history books. The area is much more shopper friendly than it was on 26 September, 1970, when all manner of traffic bowled along the streets. It is now a far more pleasant experience when window shopping or strolling with the family along the retail areas in the vicinity. Apart from that, there have been few alterations to the face of this part of the city. The building that housed Kingston's jewellers, on the far right hand corner, still sells similar products, though under the name of Goldsmith. The flagpole cum spire has disappeared, but in all other respects the dome is just as it was. Across the street, Starbucks offers its particular coffee experience. The spot where Fletcher's stands in this scene was often just referred to as 'Fletcher's corner' and was a popular meeting place for those arriving from the outskirts and intending to get together for a night out or some heavy shopping.

Right: Beverley Road, on a typical day in 1967, was busy with traffic. How different the scene was compared with 29 years earlier when private car ownership was largely unheard of for the ordinary man in the street. He stayed on foot in the early postwar years, using public transport to get from A to B. It was only with the introduction of small, affordable family saloons in the early 1950s, such as the Ford Popular 103E,

that ordinary people could aspire to what had been the preserve of the middle classes. The Popular was very basic. It had a single vacuum powered wiper, no heater, vinyl trim and very little chrome. Even the bumpers were painted, but it was within the reach of the pockets of those who started to earn better wages at the beginning of Harold Macmillan's 'never had it so good' era. By the end of the decade, Issigonis's Mini had been launched and a whole raft of smaller cars soon filled up with mum, dad and the regulation 2.4 children.

Below: The tinkling waters of the fountain on Jameson Street attracted the attention of the toddler being held above the rim so that she could enjoy the glittering reflections of the Christmas lights as they shone and danced below her. All around them, mother and child could not help but admire the coloured light bulbs and decorations that made the city centre such an attractive sight. On 27 November, 1962, Christmas was less than a month away. The push towards the great family day had begun. The Salvation Army had dusted off its brass instruments and was playing 'God rest ye merry gentlemen' on one street corner as Hammond's store piped a mixture of the Harry Simeone Chorale's 'Do you hear what I hear' along with, yet again, Nina and Frederick's 'Little donkey'. It was the season of joy, so mum and her little continued along the donkey's dusty road, not to Bethlehem, but to Father Christmas's grotto. It was worth a shilling just to see the look of wonder in the tiny tot's eyes. The colouring book was too old for her, but that was of secondary consideration. Anyway, it was mercifully a quieter present than the tin trumpet the little lad behind them in the queue received.

Left: The bobby on point duty was an important fixture at the top of Jameson Street in the early 1960s. He looked west along the road and his gaze was met by a sea of traffic that would have ground to a halt but for his skill in guiding cars, buses, lorries and bikes through the intersection. Traffic calming measures had already begun as the city felt the burden of the massive increase in the number of vehicles on our roads over the preceding decade. Just about every family now owned a car and it was used to take people to work or the shops. Half a generation earlier, the bus or the bike sufficed, but now we had cars and we intended to use them. Jameson Street was turned into a one-way thoroughfare. At least that meant that the policeman did not have to worry about vehicles coming at him from behind. Unlike his continental counterparts, this upholder of the motoring law had no need of whistles and frenetic gestures. He instructed drivers with all the grace of John Barbirolli conducting the Halle orchestra. Clear, sweeping arm movements, and an index finger of which Kitchener would have been proud, indicated which vehicles were to move and the direction they had to take.

Above: The single storey part of Paragon Station remains, with some cosmetic alterations, but the main building has been completely removed and the location remodelled. Tesco and the Holiday Inn now dominate the right hand side of the photograph that dates from February, 1975. In latter years, the station has undergone a transformation with the building of the St Stephen's Shopping Centre and the incorporation of a bus station, making it into the dual purpose Interchange. This featured strongly in the 2007 HSBC Rail Business Awards in the Station Excellence of the Year Section. Paragon Station had previously seen some alterations, though nothing on this scale. In 1904 it underwent a degree of rebuilding and refurbishment and the entrance portico was reduced to facilitate the extensions to the Royal Station Hotel next door. The portico was replaced in the 1960s by Paragon House, a concrete, steel and glass building typical of the period that was demolished in 2007.

Below: The interior of Paragon Station was photographed in May, 1979. By then, over a century had passed and millions of feet had trod the concourse of the station that opened for business in 1840 to serve the York and North Midland Railway (YNMR). This company would later evolve into the North Eastern Railway. In addition to this building, a three-bay trainshed was also constructed and, in 1851 and adjacent to the station, the handsome Royal Station Hotel, nowadays merely the Royal Hotel. The YNMR was formed in 1839 to connect York with the Leeds and Selby Railway. The following year a link was established with the North Midland Railway at Normanton. George Stephenson was the engineer for the line and it will come as no surprise to learn that the locomotives were supplied by Robert Stephenson. Well, why not keep it in the family? The YNMR was a great success, particularly in its early years when it was part of the trunk route to London, via Derby and Birmingham. In 1845, it was paying a dividend of two shillings in the pound, in line with only the top few railway companies.

AT LEISURE

Below: Pearson Park, seen in the early 1900s, was the first public park to open in Hull. It was named for Zachariah Pearson (1821-91), then the town's mayor, when he marked his term of office in 1860 with a gift of 23 acres of land for public use. He retained a parcel of 12 acres on which he built some smart villas. One of these became home to the poet Philip Larkin in 1964. Income from the villas helped Pearson to fund a risky business venture. He purchased a fleet of ships and tried to run guns to the Confederate Army in the American Civil War, He backed a loser and was ruined when his ships were captured by federal forces. He lived out the rest of his life in obscurity in a small corner of the park that bore his name. The 1897 memorial to him was designed by William Day Keyworth Jr. The park's layout was designed by James Niven. The elaborate and ornate cast-iron gateway that forms the main entrance was created by Young and Pool in 1863. The lawns and driveway were pleasant places for Victorian and Edwardian ladies to take the air. Promenading here near the delightful serpentine lake and by the pretty conservatory that was rebuilt in 1930 was a good way of displaying the elegance that was a feature of women of a certain class.

Above: The tea stall on Bridlington sands was doing good business in 1949. The east coast of Britain has many fine beaches and they were popular places to stay or to visit on day trips in the golden years of the great British holiday. The breezes could be a little chilly, or 'bracing' as Skegness called them, but we were made of stern stuff back then. With just a fortnight's break from the workplace, we were going to have our time on the beach and, if the wind blew, then let it. Men put on their jackets and hats, women their coats and headscarves and they all sat on deckchairs and gazed out across the North Sea. Children shivered as they wielded buckets and spades and then badgered their parents for a couple of pence to go on the donkeys. While they were off pretending to be Gordon Richards, the adults took the opportunity for a warming cuppa to thaw out their insides and get some feeling back into those white finger ends. Later, they would compose messages on Donald McGill's postcards that featured large, busty matrons, saying that they were having a lovely time and wishing that the recipients were here. Then, it was back to the guest house where the landlady played 'pop' if you were late for the evening meal.

Right: These children were showing the sort of enterprise that might have won them a place on television's 'The Apprentice' in a different era. An array of tins, flowers, vegetables and other assorted goods lay on the table that we presume were on sale to passers-by. A small notice board in the corner of the garden was unfortunately turned away from the camera, so we cannot be sure whether the kiddies' intentions were altruistic in supporting a charity or entrepreneurial in lining their own pockets. Whatever the intent, which adult could possibly resist such winning smiles on well scrubbed faces? The youngsters date from a time when the roles of boys and girls were clearly defined, both in their activities and in their dress sense. Lads were cut down versions of their fathers' clothing, with jackets, shirts and trousers. Little girls were meant to be like chocolate box decorations and appear to be all sugar and spice. The child here, with her hair in a bow, conformed to that norm.

Above: Standing as a beacon of cultural delight in a grand setting on Kingston Square, Hull New Theatre evolved from the Hull Repertory Company. This organisation performed in the Little Theatre, an old lecture hall on the site of the Central Fire Station. In 1924, the company hired Peppino Santangelo, an experienced hand in repertory, to take control of its finances and future fortunes. Gradually, he turned things around and created profit where there had been debt. Creditors were paid off and, in 1939, with a handy plus account of over £4,000, Santangelo moved his venture into the adjacent Assembly Rooms. Despite the outbreak of war that September, Santangelo pressed ahead and rechristened the building as the New Theatre. It opened on 6 October, 1939, with Noel Gay's 'Me and my girl'. The theatre survived the war, despite taking one direct hit during the Blitz, and continued with repertory until 1951 when the new management began to book touring shows to bolster falling attendances. Santangelo retired in 1959, two years before the bingo hordes arrived. Happily, Hull City Council took over the running of the theatre and banished the clickety click exponents. Since then, there have been several refurbishments, but it has remained true to the purpose for which it was intended. The photograph was taken in 1954.

Below right: Unless you had a name that conjured up ideas of machismo, magic or mystery, then you were unlikely to make it as a pop star 50 years ago. Reg Smith does not cut it like Marty Wide. No-one would have gone halfway to paradise with Ron Wycherley, but Billy Fury was something else. Fred Heath did not have everyone shakin' all over, but Johnny Kidd did. Anyway, if you were born Terence Nelhams-Wright, would you not have liked an alter ego? Preparing for a concert in Bridlington in 1963, this star of the pop music charts was already feeling the draught of competition from the groups who had begun to take over the hit parade from solo singers of the 1950s and early 1960s. Adam Faith, as he was renamed by the impresario Jack Good, appeared on TV's '6-5 Special' and 'Drumbeat'. Despite failing to chart with his first three singles, Adam stuck at it and was rewarded with a chart topper in late 1959 with 'What do you want'. 'Poor me', his next release, also hit No 1 and he continued to rival Cliff Richard as Britain's top selling solo artist for several years. However, his last top 10 entry was in 1963 and his star began to wane. Adam was no fool. He anticipated his decline and became a successful actor and, later, diversified into the world of financial investment. He died in 2003, aged 62.

Above: Now, there's posh. This photograph was taken on 23 December, 1949. Goodness, most people could not afford a radiogram, never mind a television back then. It would not be long, though, before this luxury became an essential part of family entertainment. Until then, an invitation to watch a programme on someone's private set was a privilege. It was the 1953 Coronation and that year's FA Cup Final that helped promote the invasion of the goggle box into all our lives. When those events occurred, people with TVs suddenly discovered that they were the most popular neighbours in the street as locals with whom they had seldom shared a conversation were able to negotiate an invite into the front room. After enjoying the entertainment offered by the splendour of the wedding coach on its way to Westminster Abbey and a seven goal thriller at

Wembley, dads were instructed to put television high on the list of goods that they could get on hire purchase. To modern youth the tiny screens and fuzzy pictures would seem hilarious. But, to those of us who were around at the time, it was a magical experience. The kids had Muffin the Mule, Andy Pandy and The Flowerpot Men. Adults watched panel games like 'What's My Line' and exciting drama such as 'The Quatermass Experiment' until the little white dot on the screen faded.

Below: They love you, yeah yeah yeah. The mopheads from Liverpool performed in Hull in 1964 and took time out to pose for a photograph with two young fans before performing their hits on stage. Actually, they could have sung Max Bygraves' repertoire for all anyone cared. Hardly a word of any lyric or a chord from any guitar could be heard above the racket that greeted any Beatles' concert. Screaming girls hung over balconies and rushed the stage, wailing uncontrollably for whichever of John, Paul, George or Ringo took their fancy. The phenomenon of Beatlemania was at its height in the mid 60s as the Merseyside sound swept the western world. It had its beginnings in late 1962 when the manager, Brian Epstein, discovered which record shops provided the sales' returns on which the pop music charts were based. The lads had just released their first single, a rather ordinary song called 'Love me do'. Epstein bought up as many copies as he could from the targeted shops in and around Liverpool. Hey presto! It worked. Artificially, he had got the group a hit that made it to No 17 on the charts. The follow up, a far better number, 'Please please me', soared to No 2 and then came 'From me to you' and from then on the number ones kept on flowing.

Left: The Peter Pan of pop music was just 19 when this photograph was taken after a concert in Hull in January 1960. Born Harry Webb in Lucknow, India, his family returned to England in 1947 and young Harry was introduced to a new way of life in Newton Aycliffe, a far cry from the home and servants he knew as a young child. As a teenager, he enjoyed skiffle music and coined a new identity for himself as Cliff Richard and formed the Drifters, the group later to be renamed the Shadows to avoid confusion with the American Drifters. Norrie Paramor was impressed by the 17-year-old Cliff and produced his first record, 'Move it'. It was a runaway success, reaching No 2 in the charts. In early TV appearances, Cliff was encouraged to adopt a mean pose and be the English version of Elvis. That style can be seen in his clothes and haircut in this photograph. But, rockabilly songs and ballads, such as 'Living doll' and 'Travelling light', gave him No 1 hits and he developed a more clean-cut, family-orientated look. Films, such as 'The Young Ones' and 'Summer Holiday', gave him such cross-generation appeal that his own television shows became part of the family viewing agenda. Still recording hit records today, half a century after 'Move it', Sir Cliff, as he became in 1995, is a British institution.

Below: The Beverley Sister, one of the most popular acts of the 50s and 60s board a Blackburn Beverley on their visit to Brough in 1958. All born on the same day, May 5, Joy in 1929 and the twins Babs and Teddie in 1932, the sisters were discovered by accident marching in a school crocodile to lessons in a remote Northamptonshire village. They were an attractive trio and secured a contract as "Bonnie Babies" in an advertising campaign for the bedtime drink Ovaltine. However, it wasn't until around 1949 that Joy, an aggrieved 18-year-old reader of a showbiz paper, sent in a letter to the columnist. No punches pulled, it started off something like: "My name is Joy Beverley. With twin sisters Babs and Teddie, we are the Beverley Sisters. We are British. Born and bred in north London. You are always writing in your column about American singing sister acts. What about us? We are as good as any of them. To prove it, I enclose a small demo disc we wrote and performed ourselves. Give it a spin, yours hopefully, the Beverley Sisters". And the rest, as they say, is history! With a style which was loosely modelled on that of the Andrews Sisters their hits included "Sisters", "I Saw Mommy Kissing Santa Claus" and "Little Drummer Boy" to name but three. They were the first UK female group to break into the U.S. top 10 and entered the Guinness Book of Records in 2002 as the world's longest surviving vocal group without a change in the line up. In the 2006 New Year Honours list they were each awarded an MBE.

Above: **P**retty girls in short skirts, young men jumping from waltzer to waltzer collecting money, the sticky smell of candy floss in the air and the sounds of Freddie Cannon or Eddie Cochran belting out hits from over a decade ago. This was Hull Fair in 1970, but similar scenes occur every October when Europe's largest travelling fair is here. Most merrymakers do not know that the fair has its origins in the charter granted on 10 November, 1279, by King Edward I, after he took possession of the town of Wyke and renamed it as Kingston upon Hull. They know that it has a long tradition and that it is an event that everyone, especially youngsters, looks forward to each autumn. Older visitors remember the first stolen kisses at the back of the dodgem stan!. Others recall smacking the wandering hands of another adventurous young man, but being secretly pleased that he gave it a try. During the 19th century, the fair was held at a variety of locations that included Market Place, Brown Cow Field and Corporation Field, on Park Street. Locals, though, objected to the peep shows and other risqué events taking place so close to their homes and, in 1885, a site at Walton Street was found. By the 20th century the fair was so famous that special railway carriages were laid on to bring in visitors from miles away. Some readers might recall the great shows that included boxing booths, the Travelling Palladium, Tippler White's Freaks, Joe Ling's Ben Hur and Marshall's Wall of Death.

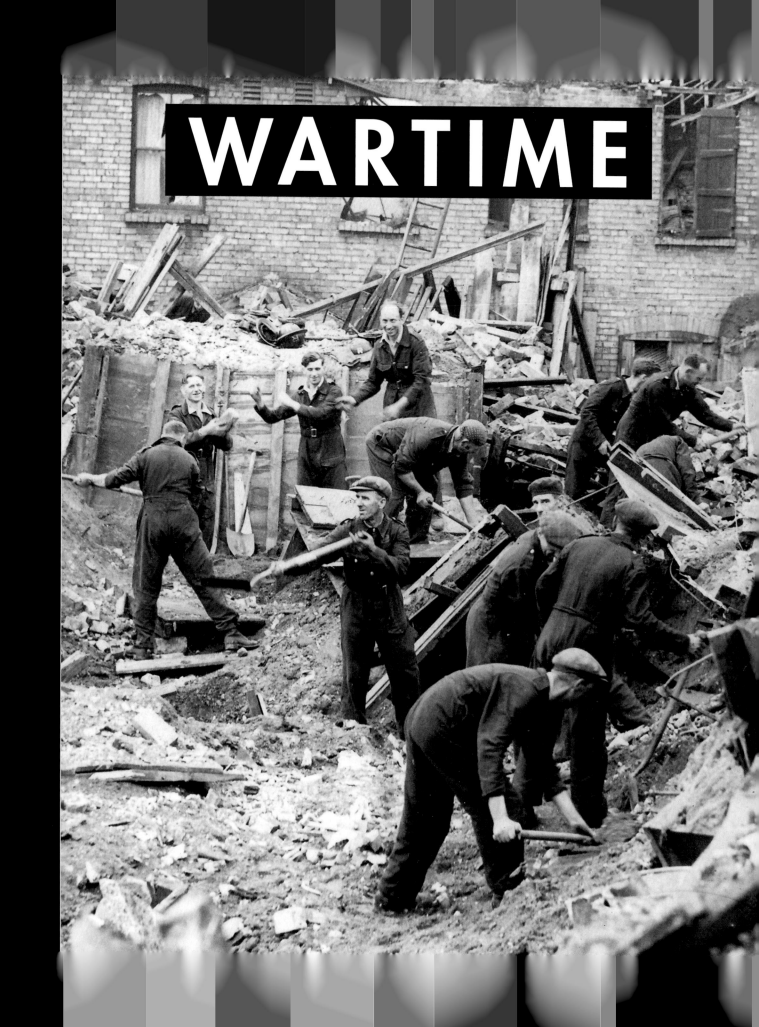

WARTIME

Left: John Betjeman once wrote, 'Come friendly bombs and rain on Slough' to show his dislike of the appearance of the Berkshire town. He would not have been so sardonic if he had lived through the bombing raids that hit Hull in the early 1940s while he was safe in Dublin. There was no poetry about the devastation that had been heaped upon Sculcoates Lane, just off Beverley Road. Those returning to the street after the 'all clear' sounded realised just how close death and destruction was to them all. It had been the incendiary devices, rather than the high explosive bombs, that had created most havoc. Householders had stayed out of harm's way, alerted by the sirens. But, while in their Anderson shelters or wherever they had sought refuge, fires raged unchecked. There weren't enough firefighters or appliances available to cope. All they could do was their best. When people returned to their homes many found only burned out shells of what had been their own personal castle. Treasured possessions and those that evoked precious memories had been destroyed without a trace. Workmen sifting through the rubble had an unenviable task. They did not know what the next shovelful might reveal. Perhaps it would be an arm or a leg or a tiny infant. Such finds were too awful to discuss and many took such secrets with them to their graves.

Below: At first sight this extraordinary device looks as if it might be some kind of early fire engine. In fact it is a vacuum cleaner. Upright electric domestic vacuum cleaners had already been around for many years when this photo was taken in the early 1940s, though many homes did not yet possess one. The idea of a large vacuum cleaner being taken from door to door was something quite commonplace in the early part of the century, and there are many pictures of such tradesmen in the Edwardian era; but by the 1940s they were almost part of history. German bombs however ensured that the industrial strength mobile vacuum cleaner was still in demand as the interiors of houses, untouched by direct damage, were covered in thick layers of dust.

Above: Perhaps it was approaching Christmas time as the men who controlled the barrage balloons took time out. One plate appears to hold mince pies that some relative or wellwisher had provided. The men were also making sure that their mugs contained something a little stronger than tea, as the stone jar was passed around. It is unlikely to have contained dandelion and burdock. But, it was not all beer and skittles for the boys in blue. Many of them were billeted far from their loved ones and these humble surroundings became home for weeks and months on end. Whether or not they took to the skies themselves, they were part of our armed forces sworn to defend our realm from the enemy. They also knew that at any moment the sirens might go as the Luftwaffe swooped down from the skies to pour upon them a deadly hail of fire from their machine guns. Then, the games of don and nine card brag would be hastily abandoned as they scurried to their posts, ready to scramble into action. The base began life as 17 Balloon Centre, being officially opened on 28 June, 1939. In October, 1942, it was renamed RAF Sutton-on-Hull. The following year the station became the home of the RAF School of Fire Fighting and Rescue. It continued in this capacity until 1959 and the land was disposed of in 1961 for housing and the North Point Shopping Centre.

The barrage balloon (pictured here and below left) was just one of the features of our aerial defences during World War II. Men at RAF Sutton worked on the cabling that held them in place, but the balloons only had a limited capacity as a defence against the enemy. They were mainly used as protection from low flying aircraft that might make a strafing run. Tethered with metal cables, it was hoped that they would damage aeroplanes that collided with them, or at least make the attacker's approach more difficult. Some versions carried small explosive charges that would be pulled up against the aircraft to ensure its destruction. Barrage balloons were seldom used at any great altitude as the weight of a longer cable made them impractical. They were used quite extensively around the time of the Battle of Britain when the Luftwaffe mounted a number of raids on our airfields. Sometimes they were more trouble than they were worth, especially when they broke free from their moorings and drifted off above city centres. Then there was the possibility that they could foul power lines and bring to a halt industry that was vital to the war effort.

Above: The Head Post Office in Alfred Gelder Street Hull was badly damaged by enemy action on 17th and 18th July 1941. A heavy raid concentrated on east Hull and Victoria Docks. The bombs dropped:- Four IB clusters, ninety-two 50kg HEs, fifty-five 250kg HEs, twenty-one 500kg HEs, four 1000kg HEs and three GMs. About thirty aircraft attacked the city and caused a considerable amount of damage to business and residential property. 140 people were killed and 108 seriously injured. Direct hits were also made on made on Rank's flour mill, East Hull gas undertaking, Messrs Reckitt's factory, Franklin Street shelter, Holderness Road, Crowle Street police station and the YPI George Street, altogether more than 200 industrial buildings were hit. Approximately 7,000 houses received damage of a more serious nature than broken windows, 1,500 made uninhabitable.

Right: Gas had been used as a deadly weapon in the First World War and many soldiers had died or been injured as the poisonous clouds were released upon them. Classes were held instructing civilians in the ways that they could recognise the different types of chemicals they might encounter, the effects that these would have upon them and the measures they could take to counteract them. All schoolchildren were issued with gas masks in the spring and summer of 1939. Posters reminded people to carry their gas mask at all times. Some were even fined if they were caught without them. It was a common sight to see kiddies on their way to school, pencil case in one hand a box containing a gas mask in the other. They were quite uncomfortable to wear. Made of black rubber that was hot and smelly, it was actually quite difficult to breathe when wearing one. Air was sucked through the filter to take out the gas and, when you exhaled, the whole mask was pushed away from the face to let the air escape. Children had Mickey Mouse style masks and babies a variety that looked like miniature divers' helmets.

Above: During the last war there were frequent salvage drives. It was a waste not, want not culture and full of suggestions about making do and mending. Raw materials were scarce and anything that could be recycled was put to use. Those of us in the 21st century who think of ourselves as being 'green', and of being among the first to counteract the throwaway society, should look back to the 1940s. Here, children at Eagley collected all sorts of stuff that could be turned into something useful. Anything from an old envelope to a garden rail was collected and transported to a sorting centre. There, armies of volunteers sifted and graded rags, bones, paper, metal and any other items that could be put to further use. Throughout the war years appeals for junk and salvage were ongoing. Sometimes we were asked to hand over old saucepans, flat irons and bedsteads to provide scrap metal for the building of new warships and planes. It seemed ironic that the Spitfire overhead might really be a flying frying pan. Not to worry, as long as it did its job. The British, weaned on a diet of jumble sales and white elephant stalls, were past masters (and mistresses) at scavenging. The skill was to serve them well.

Facing page: In 1939 Britain's Prime Minister Neville Chamberlain had made his announcement to the waiting people of Britain that '...this country is at war with Germany.' The country rolled up its sleeves and prepared for the inevitable. This war would be different from other wars. This time planes had the ability to fly further and carry a heavier load, and air raids were fully expected. Air raid shelters were obviously going to be needed, and shelters were built on open places across towns and cities. By the time war was declared an army of volunteers of both sexes had already been recruited to form an Air Raid Protection service. At first ARP personnel were unpaid volunteers but when war broke out in September 1939 they became paid staff. It was their job to patrol specified areas, making sure that no chinks of light broke the blackout restrictions, checking the safety of local residents, being alert for gas attacks, air raids and unexploded bombs. The exceptional work done by Air Raid Wardens in dealing with incendiaries, giving first aid to the injured, helping to rescue victims from their bombed-out properties, clearing away rubble, and a thousand and one other tasks became legendary; during the Second World War nearly as many private citizens were killed as troops - and many of them were the gallant ARP wardens. At the beginning of the war Sir Anthony Eden, Secretary of State for War, appealed in a radio broadcast for men between 17 and 65 to make up a new force, the Local Defence Volunteers, to guard vulnerable points from possible Nazi attack. Within a very short time the first men were putting their names down. At first the new force had to improvise; there were no weapons to spare and men had to rely on sticks, shotguns handed in by local people, and on sheer determination. Weapons and uniforms did not become available for several months. In July the Local Defence Volunteers was renamed the Home Guard, and by the following year were a force to be reckoned with. Television programmes such as 'Dad's Army' have unfortunately associated the Home Guard with comedy, but in fact they performed much important work. The Guard posted sentries to watch for possible aircraft or parachute landings at likely spots such as disused aerodromes, golf courses on the outskirts of towns, local parks and racecourses. They manned anti-aircraft rocket guns, liaised with other units and with regular troops, set up communications and organised balloon barrages. Other preparations were hastily made. Place names and other identifying marks were obliterated to confuse the enemy about exactly where they were. Notices went up everywhere giving good advice to citizens on a number of issues. 'Keep Mum - she's not so dumb' warned people to take care what kind of information they passed on, as the person they were speaking to could be an enemy.

Left: Winston Churchill made a number of morale boosting visits to the provinces during World War II. He had married Clementine Hozier in September 1908. She was a dazzling, but largely penniless beauty whom he met at a dinner party that March. Her background was shrouded in a mixture of mystery and scandal. Officially, her parents were Sir Henry Montague Hozier and Lady Blanche (née Ogilvy). Winston and Clementine had five children and their only son, Randolph, also entered politics. Winston Churchill (1874-1965) had a chequered and varied career, but eventually came to be regarded as one of the most influential Britons that have ever lived. At various times he was an author, soldier, journalist, legislator and painter. A descendant of the Dukes of Marlborough, like so many of his class, Churchill was packed off to boarding school as a youngster and spent an unhappy, lonely time as a youth. After graduating from Sandhurst, he worked as both a soldier and a reporter, but his main love was politics. In 1900, he became Oldham's MP and the love affair with power really began.

SPORT

Below: Proudly wearing their distinctive hooped jerseys, the strong men of Hull Kingston Rovers posed for the camera as they prepared to take on the opposition in the inaugural fixture at Craven Park. The team plus reserves, as this was in the days when substitutes were unheard of, were ready to grace the new stadium with its brand of exciting, but determined, rugby league. The trainer was on hand to lend assistance should anyone get injured. His medical equipment comprised of a towel, a bucket of cold water and a sponge. It was remarkable to see how quickly a player could recover from a knock when he saw the trainer running towards him, especially on a chilly afternoon. Just the thought of the sponge dipped in icy water was enough to inspire a Lazarus style leap to the feet. After much eager anticipation and the 1920s' equivalent of hype before the game, the match itself was something of a damp squib. Wakefield Trinity provided the opposition on 2 September, 1922, but had not read the script. The visitors inflicted a dour 3-0 defeat on the home side. The rest of the season was better as the League Championship play-offs were won and some silverware placed in the trophy cabinet.

Right: Freshly marked out and ready for the next session of 'up and unders' and 'early baths', as commentator Eddie Waring used to say, the Hull Kingston Rovers' ground lay in wait. Seen from the air in 1971, Craven Park became the club's home venue in 1922. Before then the team, originally called Kingston Amateurs, had occupied a variety of sites that included Craven Street, the Boulevard, Albert Street, Anlaby Road and Chalk Lane. Craven Park was sold to the Greyhound Racing Company in 1930s due to financial difficulties, but the club was able to secure a long term lease to continue playing there. It was its home until 1989. Rovers were relegated to Division Two at the end of that season and the ground was sold to Wright Properties. The stadium was demolished and a supermarket now stands on the site. Hull KR moved to New Craven Park, off Preston Road, and soon returned to the top division. Plans are afoot to increase the capacity to over 14,000 by 2010 and to include a large restaurant and corporate facilities in the redevelopment.

Speedway action from 1948/49 season, taking place at the old Hedon aerodrome on the outskirts of Hull. Pictured in action is Hull 'Angels' ace rider Bob Baker taking the inside line to try and hold off a determined opponent. The brave riders duel on characteristically spartan machinery with no brakes or gears. Interestingly at this time a specially built platform known as Hedon Halt was opened on the Withensea line to accommodate travelling fans, as very few owned cars in those days. The track at Hedon closed after only a few years due to falling attendances. The sport re-opened in 1971, this time at the Boulevard stadium, former ground of Hull F.C. rugby league team. The team now known as the Hull 'Vikings' raced on a carefully constructed track on the perimeter of the rugby pitch. The following years saw comparatively little success for the 'Vikings' despite being able to boast signing 4 times speedway World Champion, Barry Briggs MBE (right) in 1976. Briggs unfortunately, could only commit for one season and the 'Vikings had to look for a suitable replacement. This occurred in 1978 when they signed reigning World Champion, Ivan Mauger, like Briggs a New Zealander. With Mauger MBE (above), OBE, leading the side the Viking had somewhat of a golden spell which lasted for 4 years, to the end of 1981 when speedway ended at the Boulevard. On April 5th, 1995 the thrills and spills of speedway came back to Hull for a third time at Craven Park, the home of the city's other rugby league team, Hull Kingston Rovers. Although the Vikings raced in speedway's top flight Elite League in 1999, it was in the Premier League where they have enjoyed the most success, gaining a treble in 2004. Unfortunately however just one year later, the club was forced to close due to financial problems.

Below right: Two of England's most famous footballers from the days when they played with lace-up case balls and earned little more than the average working man are featured in this 1949 photograph. Don Revie (1927-89), on the left, had just signed for Hull City for the then large transfer fee of £20,000. Although born in Middlesbrough, he began his career with Leicester City just before the end of the war and stayed at Boothferry Park for two years before moving to Manchester City and finding fame as a deep lying centre forward in the style adopted by the great Hungarian player, Hidegkuti. Revie won six England caps and also played for Sunderland and Leeds United, where he became the manager. He had success with the Yorkshire club, lifting several trophies, though his side's negative and roughhouse tactics were often criticised. He became the national team manager in 1974, but failed to make an impression on the world stage and quit the post under something of a cloud. Horatio (Raich) Carter (1913-94), on the right, lost his best playing years to the war. Even so, he forged a formidable reputation as a talented inside forward with his home town club, Sunderland, and starred for England in 13 matches either

side of the war. Raich had signed for Derby County when league football resumed, but after two seasons he came to Hull as our player manager. In later years he would manage Cork Athletic, Leeds United, Mansfield Town and Middlesbrough. Part of the A1033 in Hull is named after him. Revie has no such accolade.

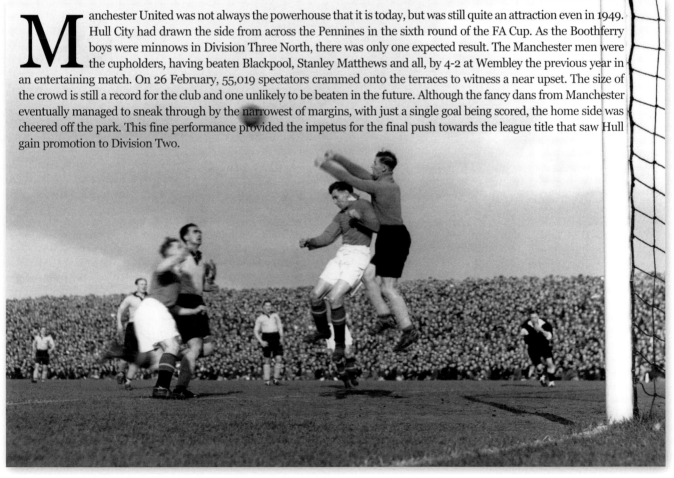

Manchester United was not always the powerhouse that it is today, but was still quite an attraction even in 1949. Hull City had drawn the side from across the Pennines in the sixth round of the FA Cup. As the Boothferry boys were minnows in Division Three North, there was only one expected result. The Manchester men were the cupholders, having beaten Blackpool, Stanley Matthews and all, by 4-2 at Wembley the previous year in an entertaining match. On 26 February, 55,019 spectators crammed onto the terraces to witness a near upset. The size of the crowd is still a record for the club and one unlikely to be beaten in the future. Although the fancy dans from Manchester eventually managed to sneak through by the narrowest of margins, with just a single goal being scored, the home side was cheered off the park. This fine performance provided the impetus for the final push towards the league title that saw Hull gain promotion to Division Two.

The Boulevard was the home of Hull rugby league club until the move to the new Kingston Communications' Stadium in 2003. The new ground has a capacity of over 25,000, whereas the Boulevard was restricted to not much more than 10,000 when the 'Airlie Birds' last played there. Hull took its nickname from Airlie Street, where the main entrance to the ground stands. Many more than its final capacity jammed the terraces and stands in 1949 to watch a game that had attracted a full house. The immediate postwar years provided a boom time for spectator sport. Starved of big matches and big name players to watch during the hostilities, fans rolled up in huge numbers to fill stadiums all over the country. Soccer grounds were full, queues formed outside cricket grounds before a ball was bowled and even minor sports such as speedway were well attended. Northern folk loved their rugby league and they squashed together like cosy sardines in order to spend an enjoyable Saturday afternoon. Hull was one of the original 22 clubs that formed the Northern Union in 1895 and played its first match at the Boulevard that year against Liversedge.

Right: Hull City had a strong unit in 1966, so it was little wonder that these men were able to play through the successful 1965-66 season by winning 31 of the 46 league games they played. Pictured going through a training routine is the majority of the squad that served us so well. Under manager Cliff Britton, the side played attractive, attacking football, as exemplified by the 109 league goals that were scored. The pinpoint passing of midfielder Ken Houghton provided the bullets that were ably fired by one of the best pairs of outstanding strikers that the club has ever had. Ken Wagstaff came from Mansfield in 1964 and immediately hit it off with Chris Chilton, a one club Hull City man through and through. Over the next decade, this duo scored over 400 goals for the club and if you think that Toshack and Keegan at Liverpool were good, then you could not have seen Waggy and Chillo play.

L to R, top: Dennis Butler, Ken Wagstaff, Alan Jarvis, Morris Swan, Chris Chilton, Terry Heath
L to R, bottom: Ken Houghton, Ray Henderson, Chris Simpkin, Andy Davidson, Mick Milner, Ian Butler

Above: The World Cup matches were only a couple of months away when Chelsea came to Boothferry Park on 1 April, 1966. City had been enjoying a successful season and would conclude its league campaign by lifting the Third Division title and returning to Division Two after six years in the doldrums. The club was also enjoying an excellent run in the FA Cup. Being one of the clubs from the bottom half of the league, it had to start its campaign in Round One. Away victories at Bradford Park Avenue and Gateshead meant that a clash with the big boys was possible when the top divisions' sides entered the competition in the third round. We drew a home tie with Southampton, a club on its way up into the top flight from Division Two. One goal was enough to take City through and then the formidable Nottingham Forest and little Southport were despatched, leaving us with a sixth round tie at Stamford Bridge. Against all the odds, we held Chelsea in a thrilling 2-2 encounter. The replay back home brought the fans out in droves and they queued round the block to gain admission to the ground. Sadly, there was no fairy tale ending and the boys from the Big Smoke won 3-1, but it was a wonderful journey while it lasted.

Above: Hull FC played at the Boulevard ground for 107 years before the move to the KC Stadium. In 1927, it was a draughty place to watch rugby league. The open terraces behind the posts were little better than earth banks and were awkward spots in which to stand. Health and safety was not an issue in those days, so no-one cared very much that it was a little precarious as there was the serious matter of watching the Airlie Street side do its best, which gave rise to the nickname the 'Airlie Birds'. Traditionally, folk from the west side supported Hull, with the east side professing allegiance to Rovers. The early 1920s were the bitter sweet years. In 1921, Hull won the Yorkshire Cup against their city rivals, but lost out to them in the county championship. In 1922 and 1923, successive Challenge Cup Finals were lost, to Rochdale Hornets and Leeds respectively. However, Hull did win the Yorkshire Cup again and top the league table during this decade.

Below: When our rugby league teams clash in a derby match there is usually some form of incident in the game that is our version of the rumble in the jungle. In this fixture from 1970, players joined in a melee after a coming together between two members of opposing sides. Unlike soccer, where sly and nasty kicks take place, the testosterone displayed on the rugby field results in an honest clip round the ear without a handbag in sight. The referee, always a figure to be respected, does not take long to sort things out and his wise and well considered counsel, manifesting itself in such meaningful prose as, 'Pack it in lads and let's gerron with it', is accepted with good grace.

After even the most bone crunching of encounters it was always a case of handshakes all round and no continuation of the argument in the tunnel. By then, both sets of players were busy discussing in which boozer they were going to meet up once they had got out of the bath. At the time when this match was played, both of our clubs were in Division One of the league. Perhaps the most memorable game played between the two clubs took place at Wembley in 1980 in the Challenge Cup Final, which Rovers won 10-5. The city emptied as fans streamed south and one wag left a homemade sign on the A63 exit road that read, 'Will the last one out turn the lights off'.

Above: Schoolboy and youth team soccer lies at the heart of the grass roots of football in this country. From here, some of the best players go on to forge a career in the sport, but for the vast majority it remains a rewarding recreation. Football and other sports play vital roles in offering youngsters the opportunity to harness their zeal and use up their energy in productive ways. They are given opportunities to develop socially as well as physically. However, they do no usually start as young as Verity Fuller. The photographer and the little one's parents must have thought that it was a bit of a hoot to pop the poor baby into the Frank Varey Cup. She will be just into her 30s by now and will be blessing her father, the fixtures and registration secretary, for this family memory. The cup is believed to be the most expensive youth trophy in Britain. Now known as the Frank Varey/Dr Lilley Under 18s Cup, the competition for this trophy is overseen by the East Riding FA. Little Verity did not know it, but she had been supporting Beverley Longcroft in the 1978 cup final against Quadrant Park Rangers. Her side lost 3-1.

Right: Clive Sullivan arrived in Hull as an unknown trialist in 1961 after Bradford Northern had passed on the young winger. When he tragically died in October 1985 he was a hero on both sides of the city, east and west. Such was the impact this Welshman from Splott in Cardiff made during his 24 years in the city that they named the main road into the city after him – Clive Sullivan Way. Sullivan 'Sully' is the only man in the history of both clubs to have won Challenge Cup winners medals with each club and score a 100 or more tries. He also captained Great Britain to glory in 1972, when they became World Cup Champions. A career in rugby league seemed along way away in his early teens after several operations on his knees. He overcame this trauma and became a winger in the classic mould, blistering pace, great footwork and an ability to beat the finest opponents. With his speed and upper body strength he was also a master in cover defence. A true thoroughbred as he showed in the World Cup final when raced 80-yards for his try against Australia which helped Britain to a 10-10 draw and the cup. He also appeared on the TV programme "This Is Your Life" and in January 1974 he was awarded the MBE for his services to the game. Having played for Rovers in the 1980 Wembley final against Hull, he won his winners medal for the black and whites in the 1982 replay against Widnes at Elland Road. Sullivan still holds two records for Hull which are the most tries in a career (250) and most tries in a match, when on 15th April 1968, he scored seven against Doncaster.

Top right: Hull Kingston Rovers have had their moments on the Challenge Cup trail, but have not made it to the last two since 1986, when losing by a whisker to Castleford, 15-14. They had previously gone down in the final in 1981 to Widnes, but the year before brought both joy and sorrow to the city. Some 95,000 supporters packed Wembley on 3 May 1980 to watch the derby match between Hull FC and Hull Kingston Rovers. The latter took an early lead when

winger Steve Hubbard scored a try and followed up with two successful penalty kicks shortly afterwards to give Rovers a seven point advantage. However, the second of these penalties came about as the result of a foul that left Roger Millward nursing a broken jaw. Wilby pulled the score back with a try for Hull, but the injured Millward, who was to play for over an hour in severe pain, dropped a goal just before half time. The sides scored a penalty apiece in the second half, leaving Hull KR as the winner by 10-5.

The following day, after an open top bus tour around Kingston-upon-Hull, the Challenge Cup was raised aloft by the brave Millward for supporters to share in the glory. Born in Castleford in 1947, he played for his home town club before moving to Hull KR in 1966 for just £6,000. Tiny Roger Millward became one of the biggest stars of world rugby league in the late 1960s and 1970s, tormenting men twice his size who were unable to lay their hands on this will o' the wisp half-back. Millward was just 21 when he became the team skipper. He represented Great Britain and captained the side on numerous occasions. After recuperating from

his cup final injury, he returned to the game in 1981 in a reserve match against Batley. He was struck in the face and suffered another break to his jaw. He never played again. Roger Millward was awarded the MBE in 1983.

Below: Pictured is David Topliss victorious Hull F.C. captain being lifted by his team mates after their 18-9 Challenge Cup replay win over Widnes at Elland Road in 1982. The Wembley final had finished all square at 14-14, and as a result caused BBC2 to rearrange their Wednesday night schedule to show the replay. Hull eventually prevailed thanks to another 'Man of the Match' performance from Topliss who captained the side and scored two tries. Eighteen days earlier at Wembley the Lance Todd Trophy went to Widnes centre Eddie Cunningham. Revenge was sweet for Topliss after his hometown club Wakefield had lost to Widnes in the 1979 final, although he did have the rare distinction of being one of the few players to win the Lance Todd Trophy and play on the losing side. Two years later he joined the Airlie Birds at age 31 for a fee of £15,000 and became a talisman for the club in the early eighties, leading them to six finals in his four years.

DOWN AT THE DOCKS

Even in the earliest of times, the lower part of the River Hull, where it flowed into the Humber, was a collecting place for boats to gather and offload and take on cargoes. As traffic increased and the size of the vessels did likewise, the Haven or Old Harbour could not cope with the volume of shipping that tried to manoeuvre through the crowded waters. An enclosed, purpose built dock was created in 1778 after the northern part of the town's defences was excavated. The Humber and Junction (Prince's) Docks were built in the early 19th century. The docks formed a type of circuit around the line of the old city walls and it was the removal of these that helped the further growth of the town itself. King George Dock, seen here in 1961, was the last of 10 docks to open on the town's waterfront. Named for George V, it was inaugurated in 1914, just before the start of the Great War. In the early years of the last century, large imports of wool from the Antipodes, along with wheat, wood and petroleum from other parts of the world, passed through the various docks. In later years this trade would include metal boxes, plastic bags, caravans and excavators.

During the Second World War, the Americans were slow to commit themselves to the Allied cause. Many of them regarded the hostilities as a European matter and it was not until the Japanese attack on Pearl Harbour in late 1941 that the USA was brought directly into the reckoning. It had, though, contributed in economic terms before firing its own shots in anger. The Lend-Lease programme began in March 1941, whereby some $31 billion of supplies were shipped to Britain to help bolster our own war effort. It was not entirely a benevolent move. In return, we had to agree to American use of our military bases in Newfoundland, Bermuda and the West Indies. There was also the added burden of repaying some of the loans. It took us over half a century to clear the debt. Part of the agreement included the building of ships for our use. Included in this programme were 13 LSIs (Landing Ship Infantry) of the Empire class. The Empire Rapier, seen in this wartime photograph, was commissioned in 1943 and was used by the Ministry of Transport War, a combination of the Ministry of Transport and the Ministry of Shipping, as a troopship. This vessel was used in the 1944 D-Day landings to good effect by the Green Howards' 6th and 7th Battalions. They left the Empire Rapier in their LCAs (Landing Craft Assault) and launched the counter offensive from Gold beach that helped turn the war. The ship was scrapped in New Jersey in 1966.

Above: A trawlerman's life is hazardous out on the chilly North Sea or up in the freezing Norwegian and Icelandic waters. He is always at the mercy of the elements and knows the risks that he takes in earning a livelihood that is one of the most perilous imaginable. However, he expects to be safe and sound when back home in the dockland. Those on board the 'Stella Canopus' could have told the tale differently. Built in 1946 by Cochrane and Sons of Selby, the 177 feet trawler had a net weight of 216 tons and was powered by a 166 hp engine. She was originally registered as the 'Northella' by J Marr and Sons, a local firm. Rechristened as 'Stella Canopus' by East Riding Trawlers limited on 25 June, 1948, she had only been in service with the new owners for a year when a collision caused her to sink. The light of her name, taken from that of the second brightest star in the sky to Sirius, dimmed somewhat as she disappeared under the water. The vessel was rescued and refloated. Later, she became part of the Ross Trawlers fleet and took on a new name, 'Ross Canopus', before being retired on 22 July, 1967, and heading for the scrapyard in the sky, or Ghent to be more precise.

Above: Row after row of fish kits overflowing with the fruits of the sea lay on the dockside on 28 March, 1956. Calculating just how many chippies and fisheries this catch could supply would keep a mathematician involved for quite a while. Whatever the answer, it would result in a substantial number of suppers, newspaper, salt and vinegar coming into play. St Andrew's Dock was usually known quite simply as the 'fish dock' because of the major activity that it supported. In this photograph we see bobbers unloading the baskets of the fish before merchants start to arrive and examine the day's catch. Some came at daybreak so that they could run their eyes over the abundance and quality that was on offer in the auctions later on that morning. Many trawlermen found things difficult in the late 1930s as the government commissioned many vessels as part of the war effort, but things improved in the postwar years and a better standard of living was regained. However, the introduction of quotas, exclusion zones and other restrictive measures in later years meant that the fishing industry never fully returned to a position of importance that it enjoyed a century ago.

Below: In 1883, the creation of St. Andrews Dock met the demands of the town's expanding fishing enterprise, though it had originally been intended for the coal trade. An extension was added in 1897. Trade and industry in Hull had been boosted by the arrival of the rail link with Leeds in 1840. Other railways followed, including the remarkably named Hull, Barnsley and West Riding Junction Railway and Dock Company that was formed in 1880 to break the perceived local monopoly of the North Eastern Railway. Despite the first designation as a dock that would deal with the transport of coal, it had become earmarked for use by the steam powered trawlers when the time came for it to become part of the town's dockland. By the interwar years of the 20th century, the railways were under challenge from the burgeoning road haulage industry, although the last fish train did not leave Hull until 1965. By the 1970s, the fish market buildings were in need of repair and it was decided to move to new premises at Albert Dock. The closure of St Andrew's Dock in 1975 coincided with the Icelandic exclusion zone being extended to 200 miles, effectively putting our fishing industry into terminal decline.

Below: Hull had one of the finest trawling fleets in the world in the middle of the last century. In 1961, the H330 Lord Nelson attracted quite a lot of interest when it was seen at the quayside. She was the first stern fishing vessel to be used by the fleet. Nets were cast off of the back of the ship, rather than the side, as with a sidewinder trawler. As well as commercial duties at sea, she was one of the boats used in the search for the 'Gaul' that went missing in mysterious circumstances in the Arctic waters north of Norway in 1974. The disappearance of the 'Gaul', without so much as a Mayday call or distress flare, fuelled the belief in some quarters that there was dirty work afoot. This was during the height of the Cold War and some shipping that frequented northern waters was thought to be involved in espionage activities. The seemingly fanciful notion was confirmed by the government over 20 years later, but a spokesman denied that this particular trawler was involved. As Mandy Rice Davies famously said in the 1960s during a high profile trial, 'Well, he would, wouldn't he?' The loss of the trawler's 36 man crew was the worst peacetime disaster to befall a British fishing fleet. Wreckage was not found until 1997 and a subsequent inquiry failed to satisfy relatives and others who felt that the full truth was somehow kept under wraps.

Right: The 'cod wars' between Iceland and Britain over territorial fishing rights began in the 1958 when the former country extended its coastal limit from four to twelve miles. Disagreements and confrontational incidents continued through the 1960s and in 1972 Iceland declared an exclusive economic zone on its waters that began the decimation of Hull's trawling industry. Earlier in the last century, Hull was the major fishing port in the land and the third largest port overall. Trawler captains shared the maritime dangers that their crews experienced, but tended to be more circumspect with their earnings. Whereas many of their workers tended to blow their earnings almost as quickly as they received them, the skippers were usually more careful. They earned more than the ordinary men, but took greater financial risks as they had to pay for their own fuel and nets. Fouled netting or a poor return of fish on a trip meant wasted money, their money. There was a distinct pecking order in the fishing industry. The trawler owners behaved like lords of the manor, the skippers like their squires and the trawlermen were the equivalent of feudal serfs. The photograph of the fish dock landing comes from 1964.

amongst the men. There just had to be, living cheek by jowl with one another as they worked, slept and worked again in bringing home, not the bacon, but the cod. A mixture of consideration and tolerance was a necessary trait for men operating in such confined circumstances where tensions could often be felt. There also had to be mutual sense of trust when working out on the open seas in all weathers as they relied upon the seamanship and professionalism of their colleagues. Fools and chancers were not tolerated. Anyone taking unnecessary risks or not pulling his weight was quickly slapped down, usually literally. If the fishermen had a successful time and the price for their catch was good, they

Above: The catch had been first class on this day in 1956 and a large example of the fleet's trawl of the sea impressed the young lady as she listened to the story being told to her about the ones that got away. At that time, some 8,000 trawlermen worked out of Hull. There was an essential camaraderie could walk away from the dockside settlings with cash aplenty to burn. There would be just 72 hours to enjoy what was left over after giving the wife her housekeeping before it was time to set sail again. In some quarters they became known as the 'three-day millionaires'

Right: Charles D Holmes and Company Limited manufactured steam boilers for ships that were built at Beverley Shipyard and then fitted out at Prince's Dock. Permission to build this dock was granted in the first decade of the 19th century, but it took another 20 years before pressure from the Chamber of Commerce and Shipping got construction under way. At last, work started on 10 December, 1827, funded by the Hull Dock Company. It was to be a junction dock between the two older ones and opened to shipping on 1 June, 1829. Thus, a line of docks connecting the River Hull and River Humber was now complete. Junction Dock was renamed Prince's Dock after the visit of Queen Victoria's consort, Prince Albert, in 1854. At the same time, the Old Dock was rechristened with the name of the monarch. Prince's Dock served us well until the time came to say goodbye and it closed to shipping in 1968. In the final quarter of the 20th century, the area saw much regeneration and Prince's Quay shopping area was built. It boasts three decks around a central atrium and houses all the usual high street names and more. It opened in 1991

Left: The aerial view of Alexandra Dock was taken in 1965. It was built to the east of Victoria Dock and opened in 1885. A riverside quay was established in 1907, south of the Albert dock, so that ships with perishable cargoes could be dealt with quickly and efficiently instead of waiting their turn for a berth in the docks. By this time, the once important whaling industry had all but given out because of over fishing. But the discovery of the 'silver pits', a fish-rich part of the North Sea, provided a ready replacement for the attention of all fishermen, not just those living on Humberside. Men migrated from Devon and Kent on a seasonal basis and a minority even relocated here permanently. The introduction of new fishing methods in the late 1800s, such as 'the trawl' and steam powered vessels, increased productivity and gave the trawlermen the opportunity to venture further and further from their base and to get as far afield as Iceland and the White Sea.

Above: If you suffer from vertigo, look away now. For those of a nervous disposition, this is a terrifying view of the city centre. But, if you can steel yourself, the scene is magnificent, showing many of Hull's important sites and buildings as they looked in 1965. Prince's Dock is in the foreground, with the floral displays of Queen's Gardens to the right. The statue of Queen Victoria in the middle of her square is plain to see in the centre of the photograph, with the Maritime Museum to its right. Until 1974, this building was the site of the Dock Offices that were owned until 1893 by the Hull Dock Company. Administration of the docks then passed to North Eastern Railways. Work on building City Hall, to the left of the square, began in 1903 when the Princess of Wales laid the foundation stone. Although it was never officially opened, City Hall was in business by 1909. The building is flanked by Carr Lane and Paragon Street. King Edward Street and on to Prospect Street is the route leading out to the top left, with Savile Street heading off towards the junction with George Street and Bond Street near the top centre of the picture.

On 5 April, 1950, the city's waterside was busy with shipping rather than shoppers or people sipping cappuccinos or café lattes. In this aerial view across the city centre, we can see Railway Dock, Humber Dock and Prince's Dock, with Queen's Gardens in the distance. Warehouses, acting as storage areas for goods that were on their way out from the port or in to it, lined the sides of the quays. Humber Dock was opened in 1809 as the second of the eventual series that would eventually dominate this part of the coast. It provided a direct outlet into the river, thus acting as a trendsetter for the designers of the subsequent docks that would be built as the 19th century unfolded. The importance of this second dock meant the decline of the harbour area in the old town. Humber Dock continued to grow as a major player in the town's economy when the Hull to Selby rail link was established from there in 1840, giving the means of transporting imported goods quickly to market. As new branch lines opened, for the first time fresh fish could be sent to the furthest reaches of West Yorkshire. Trade boomed and merchants and shipowners involved in the fishing industry enjoyed the benefits of increased trade and profits. When the time came to declare Humber Dock redundant, the old servant was revitalised and reborn as Hull Marina with moorings for approximately 300 craft of different shapes and sizes.

EVENTS & OCCASIONS

O n 8 May, 1945, a battered Queen Victoria Square played host to the Victory in Europe celebrations. As word filtered through to people's homes that the Germans had surrendered, they made their way, almost like pilgrims to a shrine, to the city centre and gathered beneath the statue of the woman who had once presided over the greatest modern empire the world has known. It seemed to be the obvious place to be. All around them lay the devastation of the night four years earlier when the city was hammered from above. Soon, the task of rebuilding the nation could begin. It would take years to achieve and there were still heartaches in store, but for now such future considerations could be put on hold. Before long, the puzzled looks on everyone's faces changed to ones that were a mixture of joy and relief. Someone started a chorus of 'White Cliffs of Dover' and gradually the crowd joined in and began an impromptu party. Complete strangers hugged one another and one group started a conga that headed off down Paragon Street. Having started the celebrations in the city centre, they began to drift off back to their homes and soon street parties were under way. Free at last.

Below: You would have thought that six years after the war had ended Britain would have been back on its feet. It was not the case. Rationing was still being inflicted upon the population and the range of goods in the shops was limited, even if we had the money to afford them, which was certainly not the case. Attlee's Labour government had nationalised everything in sight and we still had the spectre of communism threatening us behind the Iron Curtain, as Churchill called it. This was austerity Britain and not the bright country that we had hoped for after we had sent the Nazis away forever. Still, there were some moments when we could forget our troubles. The August Bank Holiday Gala at East Park was one such occasion. The crowds flocked to the grounds to watch the highly decorated floats arrive after their parade around the streets. There were brass bands to listen to and dancing troupes to watch. Charity kiosks, display tents and a funfair all added to the variety of enjoyment on offer. East Park opened on 21 June, 1887, the day of Queen Victoria's Golden Jubilee and gradually expanded over the next 40 years to become the city's largest public park.

Right: Little lads who were once part of the baby boomer years collected Dinky cars that now look for all the world just like this real life machine seen in 1949. It hurtled along the track in a road race at Brough, to the north of the Humber, roughly midway between Goole and Hull. Our collections of toy models of the real thing thrilled us all in our formative years as we whizzed them across the floor. The more organised of us built race tracks on large pieces of plywood or hardboard and glued intricate chicanes on the surface. In the 1950s, make believe Grand Prix were held and the results carefully recorded in a notebook as our own version of the cars driven by Juan Fangio, Albert Ascari and Mike Hawthorn headed for the chequered flag. There were famous manufacturer models such as Ferrari, Maserati and Alfa Romeo to collect, alongside lesser known ones, such as Talbot-Lago, HMW and Gordini. If only we had not raced them into skirting boards around the sitting room and scratched their paintwork, as well as that of the woodwork, then they would be worth quite a nice sum today at a local auction. Still, you cannot put a price on the fun we had. The driver in this photograph did not have all the safety features of a modern Formula One car on which to rely. The slender tyres, the open cabin and the simple hard hat were an open invitation to serious injury should a major shunt lie in wait.

Above: The Auto 66 Club's motorcycle sprint and hill climb section expanded in 2001 by taking over the use of facilities at Brough. It was here, in the immediate postwar years, that people lined the route as cars and bikes roared past in the pursuit of the thrills that are allied with speed. The roar of the engines and the constant danger provided an adrenalin rush for drivers, riders and spectators alike. There was little in the way of crash barriers separating the onlookers from the racers and their machines. They were able to feel the draught from the vehicles as they thundered past and such proximity to the action is probably only mirrored these days on the Isle of Man during TT week. Great solo champions like Geoff Duke and John Surtees rode at Brough, as did sidecar specialists Cyril Smith and Eric Oliver. One youngster who impressed in the 500 cc car class was to become a household name in his branch of motor sport. Stirling Moss, the best driver never to be world champion, was just into his twenties when he raced here.

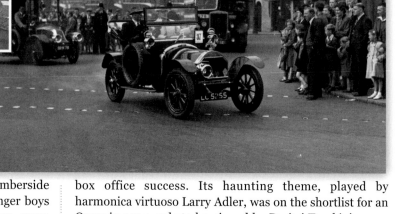

Above: There are quite a few period pieces in this photograph from the 1950s. The stocky young man to the right of the veteran car had adopted a typical look from the era. With his open neck shirt and Brylcreemed hair, swept back in a coif, or 'quiff' to which it was usually anglicised, the youth posed like some Humberside version of Elvis Presley or James Dean. The younger boys had traditional short back and sides cuts as mum demanded a good return for the tanner she had paid at the barber's. She did not want to have her offspring make a return visit for a good few months. The pipe smoking driver would probably be arrested these days for puffing away in a vehicle carrying other passengers. Wearing his beret at a jaunty angle and accompanied by suitably attired, flat-hatted friends, the rally was about to get under way. Motor enthusiasts are fascinated by these glimpses of days gone by and, even to a motorist from the middle of the last century, this old jalopy already looked to be a museum piece when compared with the Ford Popular and BMC Mini of that decade.

Top right: Another clue to dating these scenes comes from the pedestrian crossing we can see marked with studs across the carriageway. The Belisha beacon, named for the former Minister of Transport who introduced this road safety measure before the last war, blinked away without the company of the familiar zebra style markings that would later be introduced onto the tarmac below. Although experiments were conducted with blue and yellow markings, the traditional black and white came into being in 1949. By 1951 they became compulsory. Perhaps it was a rally such as this one that inspired British film makers to produce 'Genevieve' in 1953. Starring John Gregson, Dinah Sheridan, Kenneth More and Kay Kendall, it told a whimsical tale of competing couples in the London to Brighton race and was a

box office success. Its haunting theme, played by harmonica virtuoso Larry Adler, was on the shortlist for an Oscar in 1954, only to be pipped by Dmitri Tomkin's score for 'The High and the Mighty', a disaster movie that starred John Wayne.

Below left: The Queen is captured on the steps of Hull University on her visit to Hull in 1955. She is accompanied by the Chancellor, Lord Middleton, and Vice Chancellor Dr. Brynmor Jones.

Below: Looking as radiant as ever, Her Majesty the Queen visited Hull in June, 1967, to open the new Hull Royal Infirmary. A medical 'guard of honour,' formed by white-gloved nursing staff, can be seen lined up on the right of the photograph, as the Queen, accompanied by the Lord Lieutenant of East Yorkshire, Lord Middleton, approaches the hospital. Hull was proud of the new hospital which was constructed on the site of the old Western General Hospital and staffed by a dedicated team of 700 health professionals. Still on a medical theme, 1967 saw the world's first heart transplant operation in South Africa, and the passing of the Abortion Bill in Britain.

BIRD'S EYE VIEW

Below: In 1927, the Old Harbour, crossed by Drypool Bridge, was very busy with shipping. Hull was a substantial port and the number of vessels that came in and out of its various docks required skilful handling as they entered or left the estuary. They also needed a well organised management at the dockside or chaos would have been the name of the day. Fortunately, Hull had become used to dealing with such a mighty tonnage. It had 150 years' experience in dealing with small fishing smacks up to ocean going cargo ships. Although most people from outside the city think of Hull as primarily a fishing port and, nowadays, a ferry terminal, in the 18th

century it was second only to London as a port that dealt largely with imports of timber. Our town, as it then was, had a national reputation for the creation of fine furniture and this, allied with the demands of the changes brought in by the industrial revolution, meant that the demand for wood increased apace. Northern Europe and Russia exported large amounts of timber to Britain to satisfy its demands for this raw material. Before the 'old dock' was built, timber ships had to wait at the harbour in the River Hull. The old 16-foot-wide wrought iron Drypool swing bridge, built in 1888, had become a notorious bottleneck by the 1950s and was replaced in 1961 by an electrically operated Scherzer rolling lift bridge.

Above: During World War I, aeroplanes were used with an increasing degree of effect with each passing month. Technology, as often happens in wartime, moved on at great speed. Aeroplanes became weapons of war as killing machines, but were also very useful in reconnaissance duties. Pilots could fly well in advance of the front line and report back to base on a variety of interesting intelligence topics. Accurate reports on troop movements, the position of arms caches and munitions dumps, the whereabouts of supply convoys and the state of roads and bridges ahead were invaluable to commanding officers. After the war, aeronautical development continued at a rapid pace. Less than a year since the guns went quiet, Alcock and Brown flew from Newfoundland to Ireland in a Vickers Vimy machine. This was a remarkable feat, considering that Bleriot had been feted for flying just over 20 miles across the Channel a short 10 years before. Architects, mapmakers and planners realised the value of the sort of aerial surveys that wartime pilots undertook and commissioned many of them to fly peacetime missions to record the nation's towns and their streets and buildings. This photograph was taken in the mid 1920s.

Beverley Road at Spring Bank provides the focus for the 1927 aerial shot. The density and style of the housing shows that this was one of the poorer parts of Hull. At the start of the last century crowded living conditions were part of the reason that life expectancy for a new born babe was no more than 45 years, three whole decades less than the fabled 'three score and ten'. Cramped together, large families could expect little in the way of health care. That was for those who could afford to pay. The working classes knew their station in life was to do their job and suffer in silence. Respiratory diseases were commonplace. Infant mortality, though not as bad as 20 or 30 years before, was still high enough. Common childhood diseases, now cured or prevented by antibiotics and vaccinations, robbed mothers of their offspring. It was said that if you made it to the age of seven you had a fighting chance of becoming a pensioner, though the old age pension from the state would not be introduced until 1909 and you had to be 70 to receive even that pittance of five shillings (25p) each week.

Above: An elevated photograph from Herbert Ballard viewed towards the northwest in about 1965. The scene across the rooftops shows how built-up the city had become during the last century. According to the census figures, there has been a fairly constant total population in Hull of about 250,000 during that time, with a peak being reached in the 1920s. Yet, at the start of the 19th century, the number of citizens numbered about 10 per cent of that figure. By 1851, this had risen to over 50,000. It was in the latter half of that century that the population explosion became evident for all to see as it more than quadrupled in just 50 years. The influence of the building of the dockland and its associated industries is plain to see in these figures.

Below: Until 1661, most of the Old Town of Hull was subject ecclesiastically to the Vicar of Hessle. In fact so unimportant had Hull been that until the year 1301 its dead were all carried from Hull along the Humber bank for burial at Hessle. This aerial photograph of Hessle was taken in 1925 and is centred on Hessle's historic All Saints Church located just off the Square. Between the years 1868-70 the church was restored and considerably enlarged, the architect being Mr R. G Smith of Hull. The chancel and its aisles were taken down and rebuilt further eastward, the nave lengthened by two bays, and the narrow aisles widened to treble their original width. The seating accommodation was raised from 500 to over 1,000, and what were described as 'disfiguring' galleries in nave and chancel were swept away.

In the right foreground, the tower of Holy Trinity Church stands out amongst the other buildings in the vicinity. Near to it, in the area known as Market Square, is the 19th century Manchester warehouse that has now been turned into apartments. The old Grammar School is also here, a place where William Wilberforce was educated. Currently home to the 'Hands on History' Museum, the school was founded in 1486 by Dr John Alcock. This Beverley-born man was a great scholar and devout being who held many high offices, including that of Lord Chancellor. Hull's old town is a delightfully nostalgic area in which to stroll, breathing in the memories of centuries and times gone by. It was in this vicinity that the old commercial heart of the city was to be found, centrally placed between the wharves on the River Hull to the east and the city walls to the west. This is also reflected in the higher quality and larger size of buildings found here. Prince Street has a most attractive curving row of Georgian townhouses and Whitefriargate, running diagonally left towards the city's administrative centre, still retains that aura of bygone times even now.

Kingston-upon-Hull is often used for standard questions on pub quiz nights all over the country. It is one of only two cities in England to use the word 'upon' in its name. Then there are other ones about our unique municipal telephone company, the whereabouts of the street called the Land of Green Ginger, the librarian role of poet Philip Larkin and the birthplace of William Wilberforce. It also has a station with a name not to be found anywhere else, to the best of our knowledge. Pictured in the foreground of the view of the city's central area, the trainsheds at Paragon Station are clearly defined. As well as fulfilling their obvious function, railway stations have provided a backdrop to a number of memorable moments in entertainment. The 1945 movie 'Brief Encounter' was largely filmed at Carnforth and in 1970 the filmmakers shot 'The Railway Children' at Oakworth. Paul Simon is supposed to have composed the song 'Homeward Bound' at Ditton Junction in Widnes. Our Paragon Station has had its moments in the limelight. It was one of the locations used in John Cleese's 1986 film 'Clockwise'. Oh, by the way, if you are wondering about the other 'upon' city, then the answer is Newcastle-upon-Tyne.

THE WAY WE WERE

imes they are a changing' go the words of the song. But it was ever thus. Every generation believes that it is living in the modern world little realising that by the time another fifty years have gone by 'today' will have passed into history and a new younger generation will be looking back in wonder at the way we used to live in the 'olden days'. Those who were twisting the night away fifty years ago listening to new fangled transistor radios or 45 rpm singles thought that the world could hardly get any better. Wars and food rationing were things that parents and grandparents talked about. Yet so much was yet too come: holidays abroad, men landing on the moon and supersonic air travel. As for computer games, well these were days when we still made a lot of our own entertainment. And what fun we had.

Below: Here we are in West Park in 1904. Note the anchor on the left, a ready reminder of Hull's seafaring traditions, as if we really needed one. Swings in children's playgrounds are not at all new, though these early examples made from large baulks of timber have more than a hint of the hangman's scaffold abut them. But in those happy days of peace, with the Entente Cordiale firmly ending the long hostility between England and France, death of any sort was far from people's thoughts. Ten years later that peace of mind would be shattered as the full horrors of the First World War unfolded across Europe. Meanwhile the youngsters pictured here could get on with enjoying themselves without the interference of today's health and safety Tsars who have done so much over the last few decades to make children's playgrounds so safe there is hardly any fun left in them.

Right: This schoolroom photo is dated 1900. Though catalogued as a scene at St Mary's Roman Catholic High School the age of the pupils suggests otherwise, and it seems more probable that it is of youngsters attending St Mary Queen of Martyrs RC Primary School. The boys at the back are all dressed in fashionable sailor suits and are outnumbered two to one by girls in this class: the youngest seems to have got a rocking horse all to herself. Hull's Catholic population increased significantly in the late 19th century. In mid 18th century Archbishop Herring reported that there were no Catholics at all in the town; by 1780 there were just 78. By 1850 however the number of Catholics was estimated at 6,500, including some 3,000 Irish-born inhabitants. On the day of the 'Religious Census' in 1851 the attendance at just one Catholic church was put at 1,050 in the morning and 600 in the evening.

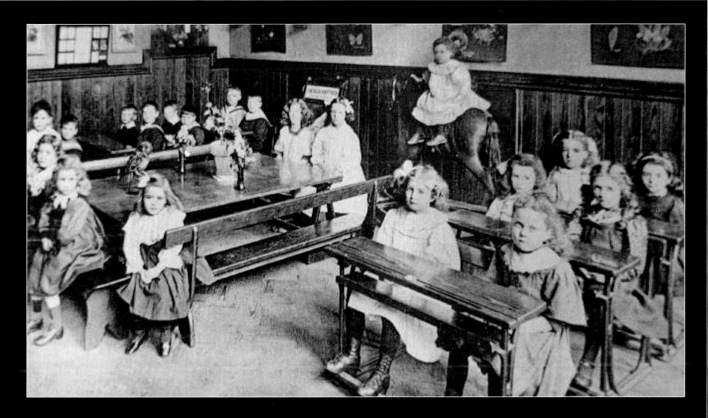

Right: The little boys in this image from the 1940s had probably been inspired by the swashbuckling Hollywood style of Errol Flynn as he rescued Olivia de Havilland as Maid Marian from the wicked clutches of his enemies in the popular movie that came to our cinemas just before the war. What would these little monkeys have made of today's politically correct regulations? Little boys were made to climb trees, let off bangers and get their legs muddy. No self respecting eight year old could face his peers unless he had grazes on his elbows and scabs on his knees. These lads did not complain that there was nothing for them to do. They did not expect to be spoon fed. They went out and made their own entertainment.

Below: Reynoldson Street in 1904 provides a perfect reminder that the bicycle age had by now arrived in Hull. The modern bicycle had appeared almost exactly at the same point in history as the car, both benefiting from the invention of the pneumatic rubber tyre in 1888 and their mass-production in the 1890s. In 1885 John Kemp Starley, of Walthamstow, Essex produced his Rover Safety Bicycle - a rear-wheel-drive, chain-driven cycle with two similar-sized wheels, far more stable than the 'penny-farthing'. Improved brakes, gears and other refinements led to a bicycle craze in Edwardian Britain. This enjoyable, eco-friendly, and above all inexpensive, mode of transport would become hugely popular.

Right and bottom right: Out in the playground or back home on the street, youngsters occupied themselves with games that needed little in the way of kit or equipment. Whatever they lacked, they were able to improvise. A game of football could be played with a bundle of rags tightly bound together, or an inflated pig's bladder, cadged from the butcher, could do the job. Games came in seasons. In the autumn, it was conkers. Cheats soaked theirs in vinegar and baked them in the oven before introducing them into the fray. There was many a tear shed when a prized 37-er was shattered by one that owed its power to a pickling in Sarson's and being heated up next to the Sunday joint. You needed the equivalent of a science degree to determine the precise moment to get them out before they exploded all over the basting tray and then it was dodge mum for the next half an hour, or else. Later in the year, we played marbles. Blood alleys, whiteys, big dobbers and stripeys all had their own special value. Circles were drawn in the dirt and

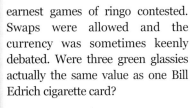

earnest games of ringo contested. Swaps were allowed and the currency was sometimes keenly debated. Were three green glassies actually the same value as one Bill Edrich cigarette card?

The school yard was a source of fun with plenty of chasing games. British Bulldog, tag and rally-o were great fun, as was the one that involved grabbing the girls' pigtails and tying them together. That usually got us the slipper, but only if someone squealed. Youngsters chalked squares on the flagstones and played hopscotch, they flicked jacks in the air as they bounced a little ball, tops were wildly whipped and two ball was played against the side of the infants' doorway. If you listened hard enough you could hear 'What time is it Mr Wolf?' being asked from one corner and 'Salt, mustard, vinegar, pepper' being chanted in another. At home we loved to make as much noise as we did on the playground. That is something that has not changed down the years. Very young children have always been fascinated by sound. The smaller their vocabulary, the more row they love to make. Give a kiddie a drum and he is as happy as Larry. Mum and dad may cringe, but the little one will have a whale of a time. Penny whistles and toy trumpets have a similar effect, both on the parents' nerves and on the scale of joy measured by the size of the smile on the little imp's face. We should be glad that schools introduce children to the recorder at an early age, rather than the euphonium.

Below: Monday was the traditional washday for many. For working class families, the burden fell upon mum. Her role as a housewife meant that the day was spent boiling clothes in a tub and wringing them out through the mangle before pegging out on the line in the back yard. Reddened hands were her reward and she still had beds to make, carpets to beat and lino to wash. The kids needed feeding and she had to get hubby's evening meal ready. It was hard work and she had few, if any, modern electrical appliances or white goods to make the task of running the house any easier. Many families lived in terraced housing, some of it back to back, with outdoor lavvies where you learned to whistle with one foot against the door in case someone else attempted to enter this little enclave of privacy. Many yards still had a tin bath that was dragged inside and filled with kettles of boiling water before family members took it in turn to soak themselves. Dating from the 1950s, this was a typical scene of life in northern towns and cities. Families and communities were close knit, sharing each other's joys and sorrows. It was quite common to lend a neighbour a helping hand in times of need.

Above: Our love of the sea as a leisure activity remains a constant, though we have paddled away on the sands in many different fashions. At one time, topless men were seen as being rather daring, racy souls. How would our Victorian forebears have responded to women peeling off their upper layers? No doubt Queen Victoria would have repeated her 'We are not amused' statement. Young women were very bold when they revealed their knees and arms to the world as their parents made sure that they disrobed and changed into bathing attire inside a machine that could be wheeled into the water. We can look back at the things people did in the past and smile at some absurdities, but we can bet that in 2100 our great grandchildren will be doing the same about us.

Below: When Ernest Evans asked whether it was a bird or a plane up there and answered himself by telling us that it was a twister, a craze was born that swept dance floors across the westem world. He also made sure that countless numbers of children would be embarrassed at weddings, 21st dos and parties during the 1990s as their parents risked hernias and heart attacks attempting to twist the night away whilst their offspring raised their eyes to heaven. Evans was a fan of the 1950s rocker Fats Domino and used his name as the inspiration for becoming known as Chubby Checker. Oddly, his first big hit in Britain was in 1963 with 'Let's Twist Again', a follow up to 'The Twist', a record that only became very popular the following year. By 1963, when this couple attempted to keep their seams straight as they girated in the front room to the music from their Dansette record player, Chubby's star had already begun to wane. He switched to the limbo in an effort to promote another dance form, but with limited success. Reissues of his twist records have enjoyed new popularity in the intervening years, but have only added to the cringe factor for those forced to watch this couple 40 years on as they take the floor to the sound of 'Twist and Shout' or 'Peppermint Twist'. Sit down, mum, it's so gross.

WORKING LIFE

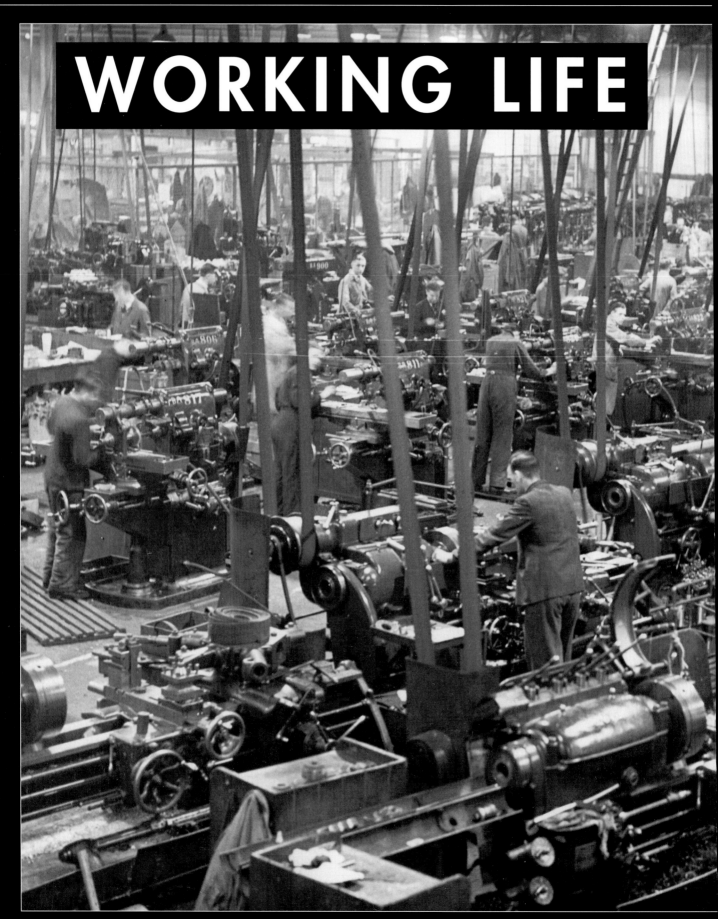

Left: Newspapers had to be careful in what they published during the last war. They were under government instructions not to print anything that was injurious to public morale, so gory details of air raids or losses of troops in battle were played down. In addition, industrial sites and their production lines had to be protected in case information about important developments reached enemy ears. Only guarded descriptions made their way into print. This operation was described as 'an animated scene in a northern aircraft factory'. We do not know any other detail, but it was the sort of scene that could have been observed at Brough. The Blackburn Aeroplane and Motor Company opened a factory there in 1916. Situated close to the river, it was an ideal place in which to build and test seaplanes. The growth of the aeroplane section of the firm was rapid and workers were attracted to settle in Brough in large numbers as business boomed. This helped turn the sleepy village into the commuter town that it has become. At the start of the war the company name shortened to Blackburn Aircraft and a number of the flying machines built there relied for some of their raw materials on the salvaged railings, pots, pans and scrap metal collected by volunteers anxious to do their bit for the war effort.

Above: Needler's was a name to be reckoned with in 20th century Hull. And the Needler chocolate dynasty was not shy in promoting its famous products. Here in 1937 are some fine examples of Needler's long remembered products such as a beribboned box of the firm's Royal Assortment. The picture is taken at Eastertide, and appropriately the display features Crown Jewel Chocolate Easter Eggs for sale at the then high price of two shillings (10p) and four shillings (20p). In 1937 at the height of the Great Depression few folk could afford such luxury items, and many children in those years would count themselves lucky to be given just a simple boiled egg with a painted shell rather than the chocolate variety.

All Change at Jackson's

Famed for its Aunt Bessie brand and with its Head Office and Group Services located at Riverside, Hessle, it is formally known as the 'William Jackson Food Group'. Yet everybody in Hull knows the business simply as 'Jackson's': they've either worked for the firm or been a customer. It's an institution, a major food manufacturing and retailing business with a history spanning over 150 years. Its shops occupied prime sites throughout Yorkshire and as far afield as the East Midlands. Its products are sold throughout Britain; it exports bread to Europe and France, and Yorkshire puddings to Canada. As a family firm the fifth generation of Jacksons is rightly proud of having adapted, diversified and re-invented itself while many of its competitors have gone to the wall.

It was 1851 when William Jackson first set up as a grocer and tea trader in Scale Lane in Hull's old town, later moving to Carr Lane. It was not until 1892, however, after his son George had come into the business, that Jackson opened a second grocery shop at 127 Spring Bank. George was keen to see the business expand, but

Above: Founder, William Jackson. *Right:* Paragon Street in 1851. *Below:* Wm Jackson & Sons Carr Lane store in the early 1900s.

jams, pickles, bottled-fruit, and even potato crisps. The bakery side had been started by a nephew of the founder, a Mr. W. E. Cooper, but its greatest coup was the appointment, in 1896, of a volatile and talented confectioner and chocolatier John James Nathaniel Mackman.

Mackman was a flamboyant man, a true artist whose creations won international recognition - not to mention some 5,000 cups and medals at various trade fairs and exhibitions. "Quality not quantity" was his watchword - whatever the expense! No wonder Jackson's cakes and pastries became a must for every special occasion.

he had other things on his mind - not least a career in politics. He stood for Parliament in the city's Central Division in 1906, but failed - despite having changed his name to Bentham to woo the Liberal vote. However, from 1910 to 1918 he represented Gainsborough. So it was largely due to the enterprise of retail director 'Bompy' Hall that the business expanded, from two branches in 1892 to fifty-plus in the early 1930s. The new shops comprised not only the traditional grocery and provisions stores, but also greengroceries, butchers, a fishmonger's - and a number of bakers and confectioners.

Having acquired a pork butcher's shop in 1915, Jackson's went into the meat trade, opening a slaughterhouse and packing plant on lnglemire Lane, Cottingham. In the 1920s they brought in a cattle-man named Harry Crawford to oversee the site. Crawford was better suited to a Wild West ranch, with his booming voice, his penchant for whisky and Stetson hats. How he went down at board meetings - he became a director in 1929 - is anyone's guess. But in any case the board was

Top left: Hessle Square, 1937. **Above left:** *Shop assistants pose for a photograph in the early years of the 20th century.* **Below:** *Withernsea and early transport.*

The Company decided to develop its food production capacity. From an original bakehouse at the back of 127 Spring Bank, the firm moved its operations to its site off Derringham Street in 1907. Over the following decades the terraced houses of Victoria Street, Crystal Street and Bank Street were bought up as the firm expanded.

Derringham Street saw the production not only of cakes, pastries and bread, but also of anything from meat pies - on one famous occasion filled with crow after a shoot had been arranged around the factory yard - to

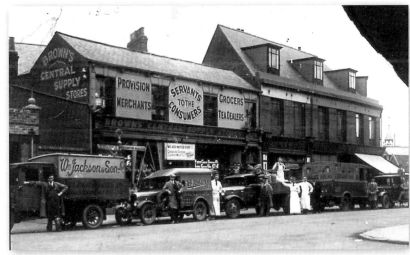

what was to be its flagship in Paragon Street: it was certainly a cut above a run of-the-mill grocery. Above the shop was a restaurant, and above that a chandeliered ballroom, one of the city's most popular night-spots.

Jackson's ran its own fleet of vehicles to serve its ever-increasing number of shops - there were almost a hundred by the 1940s, scattered through most of Yorkshire. In addition to serving the retail outlets, the firm ran a number of vans for door-to-door trade.

While the confectionery business assumed less importance over the years, bread sales continued to grow. In the 1940s Adams of Rotherham

changing. With the sudden death of George Jackson Bentham in 1929 came the kind of crisis that might have destroyed a less adaptable firm. Bentham had no sons, just two daughters - Doris and Phyllis. Both girls had been courted by young officers who served at the front in the Great War, and both had married by 1919. The young men were brothers, Jack and Norman Oughtred. Despite their personal differences with their father-in-law, they were both brought into the business.

Over the next few years the Oughtred brothers, joined the board, the extravagant Mackman left to form his own business, and the Company Secretary was shown the door – a prison door - after he was found guilty of 'defalcations admitted and proved'.

As the new branches of the business - baking, confectionery, meat and transport made further advances, so the retail arm celebrated the opening of

was acquired, followed by Swales of Wakefield and a number of smaller bakeries in Dudley, Harrogate and Scunthorpe. By the 1950s trade in the north of the region had reached such a level as to warrant the construction of a new bakery at Stockton-on- Tees.

In the 1960s enormous changes in the flour-milling and baking business saw small operators go under in their hundreds. It was a very real fear of being cut off from their suppliers by the 'big boys' that prompted Jackson's to buy into the Goole milling firm Edward Timm and Son, cementing a

Top left: *Wm Jackson & Son's flagship Paragon Street premises in the 1930s.*
Left: *Tea sampling at Paragon Street.*
Above: *Jackson's travelling shop in the 1950s.*

artificial protection of over-pricing. So successful was the shop that Jackson's had bought it out within months and, with the Government yielding on R.P.M., went on in the late 1960s and 70s to carve out a second retail empire under the Grandways banner. Grandways was a far cry from the traditional grocery store: there was no chair for a customer to sit on while her bacon was sliced or her half-ounce of pickling-spice measured out, but the range of goods on offer covered a customer's every need - from lipstick to lawn-mowers.

working relationship which would last several decades. Just as the baking scene was changing, so the retail world was also undergoing a revolution in the post-war world. And Jackson's was in the vanguard of those changes.

Always interested in new developments, the board had sent its retail director to the U.S.A. in 1945. He was so impressed by their self-service stores that within three years the Company opened one of its own in Priory Road.

After a series of experiments with 'convenience stores', 'self-service groceries' and a 'superette', the Grafton Street shop became the first truly successful, modern style super-market. Takings tripled almost overnight - even though the manageress had to stand on the pavement on the first morning and coax the bemused customers through the door!

On the back of this venture came a more startling change of style when Jacksons opened a food hall in Britain's first discount warehouse, Grandways.

Grandways was revolutionary; it took on the Government over Resale Price Maintenance, the

Meanwhile the firm continued to diversify. The craftsmen and tradesmen who were primarily responsible for fitting out the shops started to operate as Jackson's Services. This branch of the business secured such a reputation for its hotel, bank and pub refurbishments in the Hull area that offers of work came

in from further afield. Before long they were working on London Airport's Terminal Four and fitting out luxury floating hotels on the Nile!

Allied to the Services division were two other branches, Catering and Transport. The caterers, like the shop fitters, found their skills very much in demand.

*Top left and above: Shopping at Grandways. **Left and below:** Grandways Riverside (left) in 1981 and Boothferry Park (below) in 1983.*

Out of the Bakery a new business was born. Yorkshire puddings were manufactured for Butlins and it was found that these could be frozen successfully. Over time, these were marketed successfully along with a range of frozen traditional desserts such as treacle sponge and spotted dick under the Tryton Foods name.

From their Paragon Street base, they too started to take on outside work - at the Great Yorkshire Show or Beverley Races. They supplied sandwiches for the old Pullman service to London from Paragon Station, and bread and cooked meats for the city's leading hotels.

The Company already had a meat factory on Inglemire Lane, Cottingham. This was expanded to service the new, bigger Grandways.

The Company also ran a group of public houses and restaurants, such as the Ferguson Fawsitt Arms in Walkington, the pub that Jack Oughtred bought so that he could have a quiet drink after a hard day's work - or so the story goes.

On the transport side Jackson's had long been associated with Crystal Motors. With customary energy, the garages in Crystal Street were updated, tyre and battery depots were opened, and sales agencies acquired. Initially these were for Dennis trucks, Trojan vans and Lea Francis' hand-built cars, but the major breakthrough was the acquisition of the Hull Ford dealership in the 1950s. Later the Crystal Motor Group would operate Ford dealerships in Scarborough and Harrogate, as well as Nissan in Grantham and Peugeot in Grimsby.

In the 1960s computerisation was coming to the fore and in the 1970s AIM was developed initially to supply computer services to the business, but it went on to undertake external contracts for Comet and supply specialist services to the legal profession.

Following the diversification of the 70s and 80s there was quite a conglomerate of businesses and strains began to show such that the late 80s and 90s saw a period of consolidation. The last and largest Grandways store was constructed on an eleven acre site at Willerby in 1990. However, as a regional company, it found itself competing on a progressively unequal footing with the massive buying power and lower costs of the national supermarket chains.

Top left and top right: Giant Grandways, Willerby, opened in 1990. Above centre: Aunt Bessie's Yorkshire Pudding advertising. Below: Conversion of Jacksons of Brough.

In late 1992, the majority of the Grandways chain of supermarkets were consequently sold.

As it refocused its efforts on its core food businesses, a number of other operations were closed or sold. AIM was sold to the management in 1987, Jacksons Services was closed in 1993, Cottingham meat factory was sold. All the catering outlets were sold except the Ferguson Fawsitt in Walkington. The 50% stake in Timms Flour Mills was sold back to the Timms facility and in 1993 the Ford dealership in Hull was sold.

Out of the difficulties of this period though, in another retail revolution, the firm went back to its roots, developing a new concept in shopping: Jacksons Family Food Stores offering a local shop every bit as convenient as the old corner shop, serving the needs of the local community by opening up to twenty four hours a day.

Despite a catastrophic fire in 1995, which all but destroyed its plant, Tryton Foods launched the Aunt Bessie's brand, which is now famous for its Yorkshire Puddings and a wide range of traditional products.

In 2000 a majority share was taken in Kwoks Foods in Grimsby and as the company passed its 150th anniversary in 2001, Jacksons Stores opened their 100th convenience store at Blossom Street, in York, on 2 August, 2002.

The final motor business, Crystal of Grantham, was sold in 2003, but much more dramatically, Jacksons Stores was sold to Sainsbury's in August 2004. The major retailers had moved in to the area of convenience and, with greater buying power, were making acquisitions of further sites by Jacksons Stores more difficult. It was a hard decision emotionally because the firm had had retailing interests throughout its history.

Following the sale of the shops, the business continued to move forward acquiring a majority interest in Hazeldene Foods, a salad processing business in Lancashire, in 2005. During this time a major refurbishment programme was being undertaken at Jacksons Bakery on Derringham Street, which equipped the Bakery to properly serve its customers, who were principally sandwich makers.

In 2006 Parripak Foods, a vegetable processing business near Bedford, was bought and this was complemented by the acquisition of Solway Veg in 2008, which is a similar business to Parripak and is based in Gretna.

The company today is therefore the Aunt Bessie's business, Jackson's Bakery, Kwoks Foods, Hazeldene Foods, Parripak Foods and the Ferguson Fawsitt Arms. It is focused on food and on growing a successful group of food businesses.

The history of the firm demonstrates an ability to constantly adapt and reinvent itself and to recognize and seize opportunities when they are there. Its durability is based on the people who have been and are part of the business and in a strong sense of pride in William Jackson and the business he started in 1851.

Top left: Today's Aunt Bessie's Original Yorkshire Puddings. Centre: Copies of the Jackson Journal, note the seal of approval from TV Cook Delia Smith to Aunt Bessie's Yorkshire Puddings. Right: A view inside the production facility, 2008.

Wood: You'd Better Believe It - NR Burnett

Mention timber in the city of Hull and the first name which will spring to mind is NR Burnett Limited based in West Carr Lane on Sutton Fields.

The firm provides materials for portable buildings and static caravans, the merchant trade, DIY, woodworking, the joinery trade and construction industry, as well as for kitchen and bedroom units, to shop and bar fitters, works departments and public utilities. Burnett's is one of the region's largest stockists of forest products and accessories, supplying softwood timber and panel products - door 'furniture' and drawer parts, blocks and beading to clients across the region.

NR Burnett Limited traces its origins to 1935 when the business was founded by the 30-year-old Norman Rutherford Burnett. Norman had previously worked for his father, and at Hollis Brothers in Hull, both timber merchants, before deciding to go it alone.

Norman had come to Hull from Pickering. After attending school in York, Norman's father, Robert H Burnett, who owned a timber mill and timber merchants, sent him to Hull to train with Hollis Brothers Limited before returning to work for his father.

Unhappily Norman did not have a very good relationship with his father whose unbending Victorian management style eventually resulted in Norman leaving Pickering and returning to Hull. There he joined WW North Limited and became a travelling salesman for that timber company. Working for WW North Limited Norman gained a valuable knowledge of the timber trade as well as of its suppliers and customers. After several years as a highly successful salesman Norman felt that he was fully justified in asking for a pay rise commensurate with his achievements, but his request for more pay was rejected.

Though lacking funds Norman decided to set up on his own: his mother-in-law Sarah Hawkins bravely invested her entire life savings in the new venture.

Top left: *Founder, Norman Burnett.* **Below left:** *A 1952 company vehicle, pictured on a Vulcan six ton lorry are staff, Malcolm Murden, Colin Paterson, 'Ginger' and 'Taylor'.*

Above: *An ex Royal Navy Bedford OXC articulated lorry outside the company's Popple Street premises, (drawing by Ray Allen).* **Below:** *A 1937 NR Burnett trade price list.*

By 1939 a proper office was opened at 32 Clarence Street.

Norman used the back bedroom of his home at 11 Gorton Road, Willerby, as an office whilst also renting a yard and sheds in Crowle Street in Hull. There were times when an order amounted to no more than a single piece of timber; but Norman was always willing to put himself out to please a customer - an ethos later instilled in his staff. He believed that a customer always remembers good service, and that small order customers sometimes grew to become large order customers.

For the first twelve months deliveries were made by horse and cart. The following year a Guy 'Vixen Rigid' was acquired bearing an Indian Chief's Head radiator cap with the inscription 'Feathers in our cap' and painted in a distinctive primrose livery, a colour scheme which persists to the present day. That same year Norman also gained his first employee, John Hepworth, a man who would eventually become a director of the company, a knowledgeable buyer and local timber trade character who would be the perfect complement for Norman who was a born salesman. Norman Burnett's sales techniques were legendary; always a genial host he was well known for maintaining a stock of liquor in his office. Sometimes tricky negotiations would not progress until Norman had persuaded the other party to enjoy a few drinks: luckily Norman seemed unaffected by alcohol.

The acquisition of a lorry led to the need for a driver. Oscar Jackson was the first deliveryman; Charles Fearless Hemmings followed him and would later be a sales rep with the firm for many years.

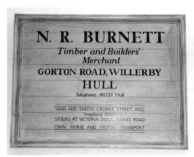

In 1938 the fear of war had led to unforeseen sales. Hull City Council began ordering timber from Norman for dug-out bomb shelters. In September 1938, however, Prime Minster Chamberlain flew back from Munich bearing that infamous scrap of paper bearing Herr Hitler's signature and the worthless promise of 'peace in our time'. The Corporation cancelled its huge order.

Norman only got his money after suing the Corporation and forcing it to accept delivery - a fortuitous event in retrospect. Sadly, however, in 1940, when the 'phoney war' became the real war the firm was bombed out and timber imports through Hull ceased; the offices moved to the safer York where Norman was joined by his sister Muriel Coutlas, who would be a major contributor to the business as company secretary for the next 16 years.

Top, both pictures: Company outings to Paris (left) in 1951 and Rotterdam (right) in 1959. **Above centre and left:** *Two early NR Burnett signs.* **Below:** *The company outing to Jersey in 1957.*

Whilst based in York the firm became a limited company. It developed into forestry clearing and, in the absence of imports, dealing with homegrown timber. Because of the urgent need for timber for repairs to war damage most staff were exempted from military service, especially lumberjacks, who moved from one source of timber to another. It was not all easy going, however, and one of Norman's first contracts would have defeated many men less resourceful than him. Norman bought 25 willow trees for felling only to find that once they had been cut down they were rotten. After considerable searching Norman still managed to make a profit by selling the timber to a manufacturer in Birmingham who turned them into shaving brush handles for the Army.

In wartime speed not quality was of the essence. Trees which were growing on a Thursday were felled by Burnett's and delivered by them to Tadcaster by the following Monday where they were planked, turned into wallboards and made into huts, which within 14 days were being slept in by soldiers at Catterick Camp!

In 1945 NR Burnett Limited was amongst the first firms to return to Hull after the war. For the next 15 years the company would be based in Albert Mill, in Popple Street, and began its involvement in supplying the fledgling caravan manufacturing trade.

Perhaps because of his own unhappy experiences as an employee Norman was particularly keen to look after his employees. In 1951

the first staff trip abroad was organised, paid for from the proceeds of the growing caravan trade. This was a rare and exciting treat. The large sum of £25 per person was allocated for the trip which took place over a bank holiday weekend. That trip, the first of several, took staff to Paris flying from Doncaster by a Dakota aeroplane landing at Beauvais and travelling on to the French capital by coach. Thereafter similar staff outings took place every two years. In 1959, for example, the firm took over half the first class accommodation on the Bolton Castle cargo-passenger ship for a trip to Rotterdam.

By 1960 the firm was employing 60 staff. New premises were acquired in Great Union Street where the timber merchant's corner site would be a familiar one to Hull

*Top left: Norman Burnett and son Barry, 1959. **Below:** Clarence Tranmer, lorry driver for the company for many years. **Bottom:** A Scarab 6 tractor, 1964.*

residents for the next 37 years. Between 1954 and 1972 annual gross profit rose from £26,257 to £117,663. Annual turnover grew steadily from £235,000 in 1959 to £566,000 in 1965. It had increased to almost a million pounds by 1972.

Burnett's was not merely an ordinary softwood timber merchant. Decorative painted wall boards were produced and sold under the Arnoboard trade name, though in 1959 that product was eventually superseded in the market place and the remaining business absorbed into NR Burnett as its decorative boards sales operation.

The 'heavy' builders merchanting side of the business had been run as a side line from the very early days, but the company now purchased the established firm of Fred Windross Limited in Hull and operated a dedicated builder's merchants at first from Cleveland Street and later from the Courtney Centre in Courtney Street. When profitability declined an exit from that trade became prudent, though the site was retained and used for bulk storage: today it is leased to national builders merchants Grahams.

Norman's eldest son Barry joined the firm in 1957. By 1968, when Norman's youngest son, Paul, joined the company Norman Burnett was in his 63rd year and his adventurous spirit had become tempered with caution and for some years the business had been simply gently ticking along. But by the time of the founder's retirement from day-to-day involvement in the business in 1970 change was already afoot.

A new team of Tom Coster (the new Managing Director), Barry Burnett and John Hepworth, together with Frank Hollings, Norman Parry and George Kirkby, now took the company forward.

However, turbulent times lay ahead.

In 1978 annual sales fell by almost a third then recovered to reach £3.6 million, only to slump from 1980 under the onslaught of deepening recession. A resurgence in trading by 1990 enabled sales to exceed £8 million. Such fluctuations made for difficulties in business planning. Net profit remained relatively stable aided by cash accumulated from years of better trading being invested in several innovative ways.

Much of the company's success in the period 1970-1984 was attributable to Tom Coster, a particularly astute Financial Director. That success was achieved in the face of some considerable difficulties, not least in June 1972 when a fire at Great Union Street destroyed the sheds. A great deal of stock was lost, although happily a new and fully loaded lorry was driven away from the flames by a quick-witted onlooker. In fact, the old sheds had not been very efficient to work in, and

Top left: Long service awards ceremony in 1988 for (left to right) Barry Burnett, 31 years, Frank Hollings, 26 years and Harold 'Dai' Davis, 40 years. **Above:** A 1996 delivery service vehicle. **Below:** Brothers, Barry Burnett (left) and Paul Burnett, 2003 (photographs by Anthony David Baynes).

their destruction actually gave the company the opportunity to replace them with new space-efficient ones.

The extensive West Carr Lane site was a major new development masterminded by Paul and Barry Burnett, and opened for business in 1997.

The firm's first employee, John Hepworth, had retired in June 1980 after 45 years with the business. An awesome figure to his colleagues he had an expert and detailed knowledge of the timber trade which had served the company so well. Sadly he died in 1984. That year Norman Burnett resigned completely from the company; Norman had lived abroad in the Seychelles since he had retired as Governing Director and had not taken an active interest in the company for some years.

Tom Coster also retired after 16 years as the firm's Managing Director and a total of 38 years spent with the firm.

Paul Burnett joined the Board in 1980 and became Company Secretary in 1984. Malcolm Acaster joined the company in 1985 and became Commercial Director in 1993 when Barry Burnett retired.

By the opening years of the 21st century the company was headed by Paul Burnett and Malcolm Acaster ably assisted by Trevor Hinchliffe (timber) Ian Railton (panel products) Gordon Lyon (accounts/admin) and John Davies (general foreman).

In April 2004 Paul Burnett and Barry Burnett brought Martin Fennell on board as Managing Director to handle the day to day running of the business.

Martin Fennell began work as a yard labourer at Howarth Timber in Thorne, then worked for various timber firms in sales and management, mainly in South Yorkshire.

Malcolm Acaster retired in May 2004 and Paul Burnett twelve months later. Finance Manager Gordon Lyon left in February 2005 to be replaced by Finance Director/Company Secretary Martin Sellers who had previously been Company Secretary for Hull City Wire Ltd. Charlie Silburn who began as an 'artic' driver replaced John Davis as Transport/Yard Manager.

John Davies retired in June 2007 on his 64th birthday after working for the firm for 41 years leaving Ian Railton, Panel Products Manager, who has been working for the firm since

Top left: Rondamat 990 Grinding Station. Above left: Martin Sellers FD, Company Secretary. Left: Harwi Orca Panel Saw. Above: Charlie Silburn. Transport Manager. Below: Ian Railton. Panel Products Manager.

Trevor Hinchliffe, Timber Department Manager and Alec Smith, one of the long serving committed external sales team. Counter sales to trade and public have doubled too – now approaching £400,000 annually, an increase the firm credits to its highly trained and knowledgeable staff.

joining it straight from school in 1977 as the longest serving employee.

Niel Fordon who joined the company as a machine operator in 2001 became Mill Manager in January 2008.

Today, with a staff of 34, the business is now run by Martin Fennell and Martin Sellers, though it is still owned by the Burnett family. Paul and Barry Burnett still call in from time to time. A policy of investment continues. A new computer and software system went live in October 2005 after five months of trials at a cost of over £55,000.

In 2006 a new 'Powermat 1000' computerised moulding machine with optical system and grinding station was acquired for £200,000, with another £20,000 being invested in ancillary equipment and tooling. The new machinery is capable of produces 600 cubic metres of machined products each month but currently is producing around 450 cubic metres a month, double that which was previously possible. As a consequence timber sales have doubled to £225,000 per month. Credit for this goes to the whole team but special mention should go to

Investment continued in 2008 with an upgraded panel saw and an Holz-her edge banding machine enabling panels to be precision cut and edged.

Today, 'Still small enough to care, large enough to cope', Burnett's Directors are delighted with the company's staff and the progress which has been made in recent years.

Top left: Weinig Powermat 1000 Moulder. Above left: Niel Fordon, Mill Manager. Bottom left: Holt-zer Edge Bander. Top right: Trevor Hinchliffe, Timber Department Manager. Left: Martin Fennell, Managing Director. Below: An aerial view of NR Burnett's premises, West Carr Lane (photograph by Sean Gallagher).

Kingston Communications
Over a Century in Communications

On 1st August 2007, the shareholders of Kingston Communications (HULL) PLC voted to change the company name to KCOM Group PLC, more accurately reflecting the changing shape and geographic reach of the Group and its brands.

The local business, providing telephone and broadband services to residents of Hull and East Yorkshire, still carries the Kingston Communications name.

Famous for its cream telephone boxes, Kingston Communications has a unique heritage within Hull. Its history and experience stretches back to the very beginnings of telecommunications in Britain.

Now over 100 years old, KC remains resolutely independent, founded on municipal roots going back more than a hundred years to when local authorities were given the power to establish their own telephone networks to compete with the US-owned National Telephone Company.

The NTC had established itself very quickly in the urban areas of Britain. Telephones had already come a long way in the 25 years since the first one was invented by Alexander Graham Bell. Telephones were first used over short distances between two fixed points, but later groups of telephone wires were brought to a central board connected to more distant stations with messages being relayed by the operators.

In the first exchanges boys were generally engaged as operators, but 'due to their inquisitive spirits, mischievous behaviour etc, they did not give their best attention and girls began to replace boys in this role'.

Switches were soon introduced so that the subscribers could talk to each other directly. These gave rise to the term 'switchboard', the first one being introduced in London in 1879. As telephone use became more widespread, the Post Office realised this posed a serious threat to its nationalised Telegraph Service. In 1880, the High Court ruled that no public telephone system could be operated without a licence from the Postmaster General. A private

Top left: *A switchboard operator outside the old Kirkella Exchange.* ***Above:*** *Boys working as operators, 1880.* ***Left:*** *An early switchroom, circa 1899.*

company provided a telephone service in Hull at this time. It later amalgamated with others and became part of the National Telephone Company.

By 1895, the National Telephone Company served 742 subscribers from its Bowl Alley Lane property, whilst only 52 Hull subscribers preferred the competing Post Office system.

However, the 1899 Telegraph Act enabled municipalities to set up their own systems under licence from the Postmaster General. Out of 1,334 authorities only six, including Hull, eventually set up telephone services.

The Hull Corporation gained its licence in 1902, on the proviso that it kept to the same exchange area as the National company. In November 1904, the Corporation, borrowing over £40,000 for the purchase of plant, opened its first exchange in the Trippett Baths building in Wincolmlee.

By 1911, the Post Office Network had 50 customers. Hull Corporation had 3,000 and NTC some 9,000.

That year the Postmaster General secured a UK monopoly for telephone services, buying out the NTC and many local authority-owned services. Hull's bid for a new licence was granted on the condition that it purchased the NTC network in the city at a cost of £192,423. It would become Britain's sole surviving municipally-owned telephone company.

A network of House Exchanges was set up around the area in the years that followed. Typically these were converted houses that contained the telephone exchange and staff. At their peak, there were 14. Some remain, but are now automatic.

On joining 'Telephones' young ladies would be issued with two aprons. A white apron was to be worn while operating the boards, and a black one for cleaning the House Exchange and black-leading the fireplaces!

Kingston Communications introduced the first Strowger exchange in the 1920s. This first automatic exchange allowing direct dialling had been designed by an American funeral director who was concerned that his business rival's wife - who was the local operator - kept putting his calls through to her husband.

During the Second World War bombing raids were a real test for staff. Several exchanges were hit. After one particularly heavy raid there was only one remaining line out of the city, to Leeds.

In May 1941, part of the administrative offices at Mytongate was destroyed by a bomb. About 80 switchboards and 2,000

Top left: *The Hull Telephone department's administrative offices in Mytongate, circa 1935.* ***Left:*** *A manual exchange which were in service from 1924 to 1956.* ***Above:*** *Listening to Teledisc in 1957.*

Aerospace had only two lines, each working on the 'ship to shore' basis.

Calls from ships were welcome because they were sometimes accompanied by an invitation to an on-board cocktail party. The supervisors took an active interest in the girls' social activities, and chaperoned them when an invitation came along.

In the 1950s, each House Exchange would keep 10 directories listing every subscriber. As new subscribers joined, the operators carefully updated the directories by hand, and at the end of the year, these would be passed to the printers so new directories could be produced.

handsets were ruined. The most serious damage however, was to underground cables. The efforts of the repair teams were often hampered by the blackout. During the conflict, about 4,000 lines were provided for the Services and these always had top priority if a fault developed.

The work could be demanding. For many years there was a minimum height requirement because of the considerable amount of stretching necessary to connect the calls. But there was an element of fun too. Friendships that began at the company often endured for life, and hundreds of couples met and married their partners whilst working there.

Former telephonists will recall the 'ship to shore' service - the operator-assisted connection between the exchange and ships, hotels, working men's clubs and some other establishments too.

These customers relied upon the operator to dial their number for them. In the 1950s, the massive Brough works of British

The days of the old manual switchboards and call boxes callers had to put two old pennies in the box for their six-minute call. At

the end of time allowed, a bulb would light up on the switchboard and operators would interrupt the call by saying: 'Your time is up, will you take another call'? This was the only time the operator was allowed to listen into a conversation, and people usually completed their call or put another two pence in the box. One retired operator remembered how a colleague had been monitoring a romantic couple for slightly longer than was strictly required. Near the end of it the young man said: 'Anyway, I'm going to hang up now, I think the operator's still

Top left: Packaging directories. Left: A new Telephone Corporation van of 1958. Above: Telephone House reception shortly after opening.

listening'. 'Oh no I'm not', replied the operator!.

During the 1950s, the Hull Corporation department introduced 'Golden Pages', the forerunner of 'Yellow Pages', for its golden jubilee classified advertising directory. In those days, categories included tripe dressers, clog makers, servants' employment agencies and bagatelle table manufacturers - a far cry from today's entries, which include feng shui, image consultants and hydroponics.

Information services were also introduced during the 1950s. One was the 'Call Father Christmas' service, which began in 1952. The concept has been copied throughout the world. The first year of the service attracted 20,000 callers, with 35,000 customers the following year. All paid 2d for the three minute compilation of a story and music spread over three nightly installments.

The success of the Father Christmas service led to the creation of other recorded information lines, such as the Telechef recipe line.

In 1967, pigeon fanciers were given a lift when Kingston Communications launched its Pigeon Liberation Service. This allowed fanciers to find out the times the birds would be released as well as wind conditions. In 1986, the service received a record 41,000 callers.

Telephone House, the new headquarters on Carr Lane, Hull, was built in 1964. The site was once the location of dozens of shops and houses, most of which were badly damaged or destroyed during the war. The facility included an exchange that could cater for 12,400 subscribers with the ability to be extended to cater for 20,000.

Top: The Central Exchange, Mytongate, in 1963. **Left**: *Installing drum metering equipment in 1964.* **Below**: *Recording the bedtime storyline.*

Kingston Communications would eventually place 500 kiosks around its 120 square mile network area, 250 of these being K6s. A K6 is the classic Hull 'cream telephone box', which was introduced from 1936 and designed by Sir Giles Gilbert Scott. Unlike BT's red kiosks, Hull's cream boxes do not have a crown symbol over the door. This is because the city's telephone service was always independent of the Post Office (which ran the UK telephone service prior to the creation of BT in 1984). Six of these K6s are now listed buildings. K6s are manufactured from cast iron with wooden doors. Kingston Communications has, wherever possible, a policy of preserving its unique cream kiosks. Those that are vandalised are broken down and used as spare parts to ensure the maximum number of them can be maintained. Kingston Communications also has a listed K1 kiosk, dating from the 1920s, in Hull's Market Hall, and a further preserved example within Telephone House.

Hull's telephone service continued its evolution when on February 17th, 1987, the City Council announced plans for a Municipal Company to be formed. The City Council had in the past avoided constraints on local government capital spending by using 'leasing' to finance a large proportion of the Telephone Department's modernisation programme. Faced with the threat of legislation that could stop this method of financing, proposals gathered momentum for the creation of a municipal limited company. Other methods of raising finance would then become possible.

The complicated process of transforming the Telephone Department into a limited company began. A new licence was issued by the Secretary of State, under the Telecommunications Act, to the Council's wholly owned operating company, Kingston Communications (HULL) plc. This became effective from 1st January 1988. The company also took a major step forward in the 1980s with the launch of the UK's first all-digital telephone network. The advantages of digital telecommunications - clearer calls, increased reliability, the opportunity to provide fully itemised bills and newer services - heralded a new era.

In 1998, the company revealed that it was to offer services outside its network area for the first time in 96 years, providing telecommunications services to customers in towns and villages across East Yorkshire where demand for its unique low cost packages - including untimed local calls - was high. The following year the Kingston Communications Group made its debut on the Stock Exchange with a partial flotation. Soon there would be 40,000 shareholders in the region, though with the City Council retaining a 41.4 per cent stake in the company. The flotation provided

Top and above: *Recording the 'Call Father Christmas' in the early 1960s.* ***Left:*** *Celebrating at Kingston Communication in 1984.*

funding for the rapid rollout of a national network that took in 25 metropolitan cities - including Manchester, Reading, Bristol, Plymouth and Exeter. The company offered businesses in these areas a range of communications services including network access, call handling equipment and software.

In its centenary year of 2004 the Group acquired Eclipse Internet, an established and growing broadband ISP that delivers internet connectivity and services to businesses throughout the UK. KC's centenary celebrations at the end of 2004 coincided with its acquisition of Omnetica, a leading enterprise data networking company, in a move designed to expand Kingston's service offerings to customers in the voice and data services market.

The following year the Group acquired Technica UK Limited, a supplier of network storage services in the UK. The coming together of Kingston Communications Business Services, Omnetica and Technica marked the creation of Affiniti, the Group's national business-to-business operation.

The Group acquired business applications integrator Smart421 and JAM IP Limited in 2006, a specialist in the area of converged IP contact centre solutions, to complement and expand Affiniti's portfolio of ICT services. In 2007 the Group acquired business internet services provider Mistral Internet to join its regionally-focused Kingston Communications business.

In early 2007 Hull Council sold its shareholding.

Kingston Communications is recognised not just as a major UK network operator but also as a company that is renowned for

innovation - from the introduction of the first Strowger exchanges in the 1920s through to pioneering the use of ADSL technology.

Today, after more than a century in business, Kingston Communications' ambition is to be the number one choice in the UK for the provision of voice, data and video communications and related services.

Meanwhile Hull's telephone system remains unique. Kingston Communications, the former Hull Telephone Department, operates one of Europe's most advanced telephone networks, serving some 185,000 customers across its East Yorkshire network. Also unique is the company's pricing policy. Socially-orientated tariffs have resulted in one of the highest penetrations of telephone users in the UK, some 94 per cent of households having access to a telephone.

Above: An engineer jointing a 1200 pair telephone cable.
Below left: Kingston Communications' famous K6 kiosks.
Below: The first stages of Kingston's network expansion outside its traditional boundaries.

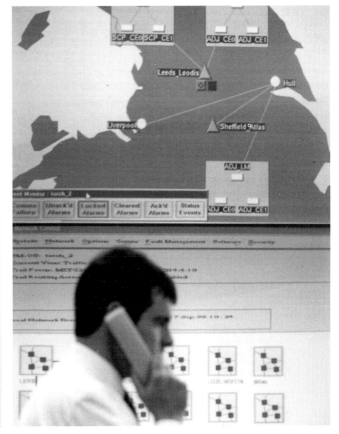

Sandhill Nurseries and Garden Centre
A Growing Business

In 1940 John Reuben Johnson (known affectionately as Reuben) was working at Tommy Howells' market garden in Preston just to the east of Hull. Whilst working there he gained his City & Guilds in horticulture at night school. He was also a sergeant in the Home Guard, getting ready to repel the expected invasion by Hitler's forces, who threatened to swarm across the North Sea following the evacuation of the British Army from Dunkirk in the last week of May and the first week of June.

Yet Reuben had an ambitious dream far removed from thoughts of war and its attendant hazards. The ultimate fruit of Reuben's ambition is today's well known Sandhill Nurseries and Garden Centre, based in Wyton Road, Preston.

Today Sandhill offers customers everything from bedding plants to water barrels, garden tools to fertilisers and chemicals, propagators to hanging baskets, giftware to Wellington boots, garden irrigation to spring bulbs, seeds to laundry accessories and from rainwear to sunhats as well as a vast range of other products.

Things started much more simply however.

Reuben married Mary Longman in 1942 and two years later, in February 1944, he bought a market garden of one acre along with a small wooden bungalow: it cost just £400. The bungalow was called Sandhill, which is where today's garden centre got its name. The previous owners had named it Sandhill as the land had belonged to the council before them; it was used to store sand and grit to repair the roads.

There were piggeries and goats on the land and Reuben grew celery, chrysanthemums and a variety of other cut flowers.

Reuben and Mary's son Kevin was born at Sandhill in July 1944, and daughter Wendy followed in 1946.

By the time Wendy was born the first growing greenhouse had already been erected on the site and by 1948 a house had also been built.

Business was increasing by then, and Reuben had begun renting another 13 acres across the road, where cut flowers, soft fruits and vegetables were grown. Soon after the first greenhouse was built on this site from which the finest cinerarias were produced.

*Above: Reuben Johnson. **Below left:** Reuben on the nursery in the early days. **Below:** The original house built in 1948.*

Sandhill was renowned for its strawberries from the late 1940s to the early 1970s. Many who ate them during those days are still mourning the ending of 25 years of growing quality strawberries.

In 1949 the expanding firm acquired a shop on Holderness Road, which became a general greengrocers, selling some of the stock grown at Sandhill. But though vegetables may have been doing well it was the trade in flowering plants that was blooming: in 1950 the firm produced 30,000 cinerarias in one year, which were sold to wholesale markets all over the north of England and the Midlands.

The Holderness Road shop was sold in 1951 and another shop on Cottingham Road was bought. This shop too sold vegetables and flowers. Reuben and his family lived above this shop for the next six years until in 1957 the family moved back to the house at Sandhill.

At Sandhill there would be many changes in the following years. In 1958 what became known as the 'Big Shed' was built at the nurseries on part of the rented land.

The first garden centre greenhouse was built in 1964. It cost £1,000 and was located where the coffee shop is now. The builder told Reuben that he thought he was wasting his money as there would be no future in what he was doing!

Despite that gloomy prophesy the garden centre, which was the first in the area and one of only a few in the UK, opened in 1965. Massive quantities of bedding plants were sold in those early days, plants which had previously been sold in the Humber Street Market.

A European dimension came to the business in 1968. In October that year a container arrived from Holland filled with young plants, trees and shrubs. They were looked after and 'potted on' in the nursery, then brought across to retail in the correct seasons. This shipment continued every October for many years.

The front and middle of the shop were built (where the farm shop and the run up to the tool department is today) in 1970. The plant house was moved to the front and the old plant house became a pet product department - although not selling animals.

Top: *Early strawberry picking.* ***Left:*** *The first greenhouse, situated where the coffee shop stands today.*

Three acres were bought from a Mr. Garbutt in 1971 and the right of way was moved to where it is today. The bank manager (another sceptic) tried to stop Reuben from spending his money on the extra land as he believed it was a waste of cash. But Reuben had a vision and he was very determined to see it come to fruition.

In 1971 Kevin Johnson came back to Sandhill from teaching, and married his wife Sally in August at Snaith, where Sally had formerly lived, and where the couple first met. By then roses were the big thing. The 1971 Roses catalogue indicates the range and volume of roses sold: in particular the firm's '10 for £1' second-grade roses sold about 40,000 each year.

In the mid-1970s the garden centre was visited on several occasions by Percy Thrower, Britain's best-known gardener, horticulturist, broadcaster and writer. These were open days organised by ICI.

The business bought the land across the road in 1973, some of which had previously been rented, along with four more acres on the garden centre side: this would eventually become the Planteria department.

In 1979 Reuben also bought the land on which Pets R Wright now stands. Until then Reuben had been sole proprietor of the firm, but in 1980 that was to change when Reuben and his son Kevin became partners.

Top: Percy Thrower visits Sandhill in the 1970s. **Above:** *Sandhill's first inspirational Christmas display.* **Left:** *Sandhill Country Park land, purchased in 1991.*

Marking the new partnership another greenhouse was built for bedding plants (this is today's houseplant/floristry greenhouse). In 1982 a netted area was created on the four acres which had been bought in 1973 on which shrubs and conifers were stored: they were brought out into retail areas of the garden centre a few at a time. A year later this area was opened to the public to walk round. The netting was up for about five years before being taken down, and the area opened up to create the planteria, though this was subject to a few years of development and changes.

Reuben visited Thailand in 1982 to look at silk flowers, and he considered bringing container loads back, but this did not prove practical. However as a result of the Thailand visit, where the idea came from, in 1983 Sandhill started selling Christmas decorations. That same year a Tearoom opened which was run directly by Sandhill for about a year before being rented out.

Sadly in 1984 the firm's founder, Reuben Johnson, passed away.

Steve Sweetman (currently Giftware & Outdoor Living Manager), who already worked at Sandhill and had done so since leaving school, began helping Kevin run the business.

During the following 12 months Kevin got involved in sports, Preston Boys FC, who used to practise on the car park (where Pets R Wright is now) and played their matches at South Holderness School. His involvement with table tennis started during this period too, because it was a game that Kevin could play at night (as he worked 12 hours a day, seven days a week!)

The following years would be busy ones. In 1986 the Nursery retail greenhouse was built for bedding plants. Some 32 acres of land was purchased across the road in 1991, this became the Sandhill Country Park. The next year Ashlyn farm was purchased, which consisted of 37 acres.

Some changes were inevitable. Everything was unloaded by hand until a forklift was purchased, Kevin put off buying the forklift because he thought it was a waste of money.

Sally Johnson, Kevin's wife, started doing inspirational Christmas displays in 1992. Two years later the pet shop was built and rented out to Ray Wright, trading as Pets R Wright.

Top: *Unloading thousands of Christmas trees by hand.* **Below left:** *Dean Windass of Hull City AFC presenting Kevin Johnson with an award for his Football in the Community work, 1995.* **Below:** *Kevin with the Hull Sandhill women's table tennis team, 1992.*

Reuben's widow, Mary Johnson, died in 1994. That same year Kevin rented a shop in Anlaby called " Sandhill Gifts and Gardens", whilst his son Steve started working at Sandhill.

Young Steve Johnson had once created a den on the Sandhill site, though no-one knew it was there: it was so well hidden that the tractor was driven into it!

Steve clearly took after his father, because a young Kevin had once made an underground den across the road. He left a small fire burning in it whilst he went home to watch football on television (Aston Villa V Manchester United at Wembley), because his dad Reuben had gone to see the match. When he came back the whole den was on fire.

In later years when Kevin went on holiday the staff used to take the opportunity to have a good clean up and have a bonfire to get rid of all the rubbish. It happened so often it got to the point where Kevin would tell them before he went away what they were allowed to burn!

Meanwhile the first broadcasting of 'Ground Force' in 1997, and other garden makeover shows that followed, had a huge effect on garden centres; gardening became fashionable. During the eight years the show was on air people started buying more and more unusual garden products trying to recreate the designs from the programme.

In 1999 having just overseen the building of a new greenhouse built on the nursery Kevin retired - for the first time! He would come back in 2004.

Top: David Bellamy pictured on his visit in 2002. **Left:** *The new coffee shop opened in 2007 on the site of the very first garden centre greenhouse.* **Below:** *The children's play area also opened in 2007.*

Before Kevin's official return from retirement Sandhill was visited in 2002 by David Bellamy the famous botanist, author, broadcaster and environmental campaigner. This was to promote selling Third World products and giving them a fair price. The project was called 'And Albert', also known as 'Trading Roots'.

Kevin retired for a second time in 2006. As a consequence Steve Pontone was appointed managing director and set about planning a refurbishment programme.

Poly-tunnels were opened in 2007, allowing customers to shop for outdoor plants whatever the weather. That same year a Farm Shop appeared, a new coffee shop opened where floristry had previously been located, and a play area and animal farm created. It really was a case of 'all change' in 2007. An all-year-round Christmas room opened, whilst major refurbishment of the clothing department, Floristry/houseplants, Garden care, Aquatics, Tools, and Giftware took place.

In 2008 show gardens were completed. Crazy golf arrived too. The frontage was refurbished and plans laid for even more changes, including a purpose-built cafe/restaurant. Sandhill were presented in July with a national garden trade show award for their show gardens and crazy golf course. Glee is the largest annual trade event for the garden, pet and leisure industries and each September, 22,000 trade visitors meet at the NEC Birmingham, over three days, making it the industry's favourite place to do business and where, needless to say, Sandhill begins formulating its plans for the following season.

As for visitors to Sandhill, whether customers are starting from a bare area of earth, just looking for ideas to enhance an existing established garden, or simply want a spring makeover, the business can provide the inspiration, the product and the expertise.

Today's business is much more then just a simple garden centre. If customers want to fit out a conservatory, Sandhill can provide the cane furniture, the plants - from orchids to bonsai, citrus to carnivorous, cacti to succulents - the pots, the wind chimes, the ornaments, and even the designer mugs for a better tasting cup of coffee.

Want to build a patio with shimmering stone paving, earthenware pots, surrounded by topiary or climbers, conifers or alpines, where sizzling delicacies are prepared on your own gas BBQ and savoured on a fine quality outdoor dining suite? You can at Sandhill.

As for those needing to mark a special occasion with a greeting card, a gift, gift-wrap or a teddy, candles or Belgian chocolates, flowers or silver jewellery Sandhill has something for everyone. And that even includes indoor furniture, from kitchen to lounge, coasters and placemats, serviettes and cushions, pictures and

rugs and vases. Visitors who want to relax can stroll through the lovingly cared for plants and shrubs, listening to the trickle of water as it falls down the granite obelisk water feature lit by solar outdoor lighting.

The Sandhill team prides itself on providing first class customer service where inspiration and variety are all in one shopping experience.

Today Sandhill remains in family ownership, as it has done since the firm was founded by Reuben Johnson in those long ago days in the 1940s.

Top left: *Crazy golf, opened in 2008.* **Above:** *The show gardens also opened in 2008.* **Left:** *Phil Readymartcher Planteria Manager and assistant John Wymark being presented with the Garden Trade Show award in July 2008.*

EYMS Group Ltd - A Full Circle of Service

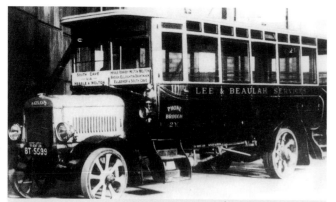

Numbered 5 in the new EY fleet this is a 1922 Leyland G7 with Leyland 26 seat body

East Yorkshire Motor Services Ltd was registered in October 1926 by the British Automobile Traction Co Ltd when it took over Lee & Beulah Ltd and Hull & District Motor Services Ltd. Starting with a fleet of some 34 buses, the new company adopted Lee & Beulah's colours of indigo and primrose. By the end of that month four more operators had been taken over, one of them David William Burn who had moved to Hull and started a cycle building and repair shop which he ran in West Parade in the 1920s. 'East Yorkshire' quickly began to establish itself as a major operator in the Hull area. Before the year ended the company took delivery of its first brand new buses, five 31-seater Leylands.

A property at Anlaby Common was acquired for offices and workshops; soon services had been established to York. By 1927 larger offices were needed and accommodation was rented in Leyton Chambers in Paragon Street. Those offices remained in use until May 1941 when they were badly damaged in one of the many bombing raids on Hull. Also in 1927 Lister Street Garage was purchased for £4,500 to house the company's fleet. By now it was operating 16 routes, most of which radiated from Hull. Eleven more new Leyland buses were ordered, and more local operators were taken over including such well-known names as Laidlaws of Hedon, Holts of Newport, Fussey of Cottingham and Jacksons of Aldbrough

By 1929 the company had already outgrown the Lister Street premises and property was acquired on Anlaby Road, including

Top left: *This magnificent vehicle was in at the birth of EYMS in 1926. It was in the fleet of Lee & Beulah, one of the two operators which joined forces to form East Yorkshire. It later became a lorry with CA and FV Coote of Hull and lasted until 1937.* **Below:** *This TD3 is seen outside the East Yorkshire offices in Paragon Street, Hull, which were blitzed in 1941.*

1934 Leyland 'Titan' TD3 Brush 52 seat body

1934 Leyland 'Tiger' TS6 English Electric 31 seat coach body

records. Surprisingly few of East Yorkshire's vehicles were damaged because of a scheme to park them on the streets away from the garage.

Expansion continued after the war. In the 1950s Crosby's of Hunmanby, Williamson's and White Bus Service, both of Bridlington, and Everingham Brothers of Pocklington were purchased.

During 1950 East Yorkshire experimented with changes of livery, but soon went back to indigo and primrose. In 1969 East Yorkshire, by then part of the national BET Group, became a subsidiary of the National Bus Company when BET sold its bus and coach interests to the Government. NBC decided

Above: This bus was withdrawn in 1950 and sold to a travelling showman. Note the driver loading luggage on the roof rack. Left: Pictured on the EY bus park (always known to EY staff as 'the Muck'!) behind the old Hull bus station, this was one of the many buses built to the standard wartime 'utility design required by the government to save materials but still with the necessary Beverley Bar roof for East Yorkshire. Below: This picture clearly shows the reason for the unique design of most EYMS double decks from 1934 to 1971, although, towards 1960 the lower buses available did not need quite such modifications.

1942 Leyland 'Titan' TD7 Brush 56 seat body

an imposing building known as Marlborough House at the junction with Arnold Street, and the former Holy Trinity Vicarage at 252 Anlaby Road. Marlborough House was demolished and a large garage was built to house and maintain the expanding fleet. The garage remains the company's main operating depot today, and 252 Anlaby Road is still the EYMS head office address, although the offices now extend over the four adjacent houses. Additional land bought at various times at the rear of the garage provides parking for today's much larger fleet.

Another major development also took place in 1929 when a new express service from Hull to Blackpool was started, together with a service to Birmingham. These services were maintained using new Leyland 'Tiger' coaches.

Acquisitions continued during the Thirties with Blue Bus Service of Bridlington, H C Motor Works and Binnington's, both of Hull, and one or two others all becoming part of EYMS. By 1933 East Yorkshire was operating 145 buses and coaches over 36 routes. The next year 34 new buses and coaches joined the fleet, some with the top deck tapered inwards to allow for the Gothic arch of Beverley Bar, under which many vehicles had to pass on their way to Hull. This remained a unique feature of almost all EYMS double-deck buses until 1971 when the Bar was by-passed.

Disaster struck in 1941 when enemy action destroyed Leyton Chambers, together with most of the company

1950 Leyland 'Titan' PD2/3 Roe 56 seat body, withdrawn in 1966

1952 Leyland 'Titan' PD2/12 Roe 50 seat body designed for long distance routes

to impose a standard colour scheme on all its bus fleets. Subsidiary companies were given the option of either poppy red and white, or leaf green and white. EYMS managed to get away with a dark blue and white scheme for a short while before being forced into line in 1972 when it reluctantly adopted the red and white option.

The Conservative Government of the eighties decided to reverse the nationalisation decision of the Labour Government of the sixties, and set about privatising the seventy-plus subsidiaries of the National Bus Company.

A management buyout of the company was completed in February 1987. A new company, EYMS Limited (later to become EYMS Group Limited) was formed for the purpose of acquiring East Yorkshire Motor Services. The sale also included the Scarborough area operations of the much larger NBC subsidiary United Automobile Services Ltd. The former United services became 'Scarborough and District' under EYMS ownership. East Yorkshire's new owners decided to stay with red as the fleet colour, although it was soon modified to a more attractive deeper red and cream. Later still it was developed into the attractive burgundy and cream livery which identifies EYMS buses today. At least one bus however, always operates in the traditional indigo and primrose colours.

Cherry Coaches of Anlaby was acquired in the mid-1980s, Metro Coaches and Rhodes Coaches, in the early 1990s. In 1988 East Yorkshire bought eight former London Transport 'Routemaster' double-deck buses with traditional open rear platforms, painted them in the old indigo and primrose colours and put them into service, complete with conductors, on route 56 which included the whole length of the busy Holderness Road on its way between the city centre and Longhill Estate. The Routemasters were an instant success, and led to another twelve being bought for new EYMS routes to the northern part of the city. The year 1988 also brought a new minibus service between Beverley and Hull. Less happily a two-week strike occurred during the annual

1974 Leyland Atlantean AN68/1R Park Royal 73 seat body

Top: *Photographed in 1958 on Beverley Road, Hull, this and several similar buses were painted in the Primrose and Riviera Blue coach colours and known to staff as the 'Yellow perils'!* ***Above:*** *This type became one of the 'standard' buses ordered in large numbers for NBC companies in the 1970s.*

Volvo 610

wage negotiations! This was the first significant industrial action since 1936. Generally the company has enjoyed a history of excellent industrial relations - a situation which fortunately continues today.

The coach fleet, which had dwindled significantly during NBC ownership, expanded since privatisation and now reverted to the original East Yorkshire coach colours of Riviera blue and primrose, though with the addition of a burgundy and cream 'kite' logo to suggest freedom and to emphasise the link to the company's successful bus operations.

In 1992 the Group made its most significant acquisition – Finglands Coachways – which ran about 50 buses and coaches in South Manchester. Then in September 1997 came a return to family ownership, as over the intervening years all save one member of the 1987 buyout team had left through retirement or to follow other interests. This left Peter Shipp, who had been at EYMS since 1980, first as Traffic Manager and later as Chairman, as the sole shareholder following a 'demerger' of the main coaching arm - National Holidays – which the last remaining other shareholder took away from the Group as part of the sale of his stake in the company.

Another significant move came in 2004: the purchase of the privately-owned operator Whittle's Coaches, a 50-vehicle operator based in Kidderminster which coincidentally also started business in 1926. Re-named Whittle Coach & Bus Ltd. this is thus now part of the Group, which runs a total of 440 buses and coaches, employs around 950 people and in 2007 had a turnover of more than £37 million.

Not bad progress for a company which almost ceased to exist as a separate entity under NBC ownership in the mid-eighties. By that time,

due to service reductions of the previous few years because of Government funding cuts, and big passenger losses, the fleet size had shrunk to just 153 vehicles making East Yorkshire a candidate for merger with NBC's Lincolnshire subsidiary, the opening of the Humber Bridge having made this a practical possibility.

Today EYMS is one of only two of the former NBC companies to remain independent and privately-owned, most of the other seventy having been bought by what are now the 'big five' bus groups.

In private ownership EYMS has made determined efforts to improve the quality of its services and has invested heavily in staff training, and in ensuring that its fleet of buses and coaches is as up-to-date as possible, a policy demonstrated by spending of £25 million on new buses and coaches between 1999 and 2007.

Having successfully passed from private enterprise, through membership of a large national group, and then state ownership, the company completed the full circle back into the private sector. In 1997 it returned to sole family ownership some 71 years after starting life in a Hull back street. The East Yorkshire company celebrated its 80th anniversary in 2006 with confidence in its next 80 years.

Top left: *To celebrate EYMS' 75th anniversary this bus was painted on one side and the rear in indigo and primrose and the front and nearside in the current colours of burgundy and cream.* ***Below:*** *One of 20 Volvo's delivered to EYMS in 2008. This bus is pictured on the forecourt of the Elloughton depot which is the exact location of the former Lee and Beulah garage, where it all began in 1926.*

Volvo B9TL chasis with Wrightbus Eclipse Gemini double-deck wheelchair-accessible body

G F Smith & Son - A Historic Paper Trail

Today GF Smith & Son of Hull is Europe's leading specialty supplier of fine, coloured, textured and unusual papers. The company has been recognised internationally for its inspiration, creativity, and quality for over a century.

In the 1880s and 1890s Mr George Frederick Smith and his brother Mr Thomas James Smith ran two small businesses from premises in North Church Side in Hull.

Thomas Smith sold cod liver oil and surgical dressings whilst his brother George sourced and distributed fine papers to commercial artists and printers in the UK.

George had two sons, Thomas Brooke Smith and Horatio Nelson Smith. Thomas Brooke Smith worked with his father and their company became known as G F Smith & Son Paper Merchants: Horatio Nelson worked for his uncle, Thomas James Smith, an arrangement which eventually led to the creation of the famous firm of TJ Smith & Nephew Ltd.

It was Thomas Brooke Smith however, who was instrumental in the rapid growth of the paper company, being responsible for sourcing products, a task which included travelling to the United States and successfully securing the British and European rights

Top left: *George Frederick Smith.* **Left:** *Horatio Nelson Smith.* **Above:** *Thomas Brooke Smith.* **Facing page:** *The devastation caused to GF Smith & Sons during the bomings of May 1941.*

to sell the exclusive papers of one of America's finest paper producer. As a result of that exploratory journey to America an exclusive business partnership was born between GF Smith and a leading paper mill, The Strathmore Paper Company - a specialist manufacturer of exquisite fine papers. A flourishing trade began, which due to hard work, single focus and a creative diligence continues to thrive to this day despite the disasters which lay ahead of the fledgling firm in the first half of the 20th century.

TJ Smith & Nephew saw a dramatic change in fortunes during the First World War. They supplied surgical dressings and bandages to the British, French, American and Canadian armies. This helped Smith & Nephew on the road to becoming the international pharmaceutical giant that it is today.

The Great War was not quite so kind to GF Smith & Son. With paper stocks held throughout Europe, which with the advent of the war it was unable to access or sell, the company was left with a large debt to its American supplier which it could not pay.

As the American supplier had great confidence in the longer term post-war potential of the company and its ability to sell American products, the supplier agreed to take over GF Smith & Son. One of the company's managers, Mr HE Thomlinson was appointed to act as Managing Director and

look after the supplier's UK interests. Sadly from that point the Smith family had no further involvement in the firm.

GF Smith & Son was successfully rebuilt after the Great War and it acquired new premises in Osbourne Street, Hull. The larger premises facilitated more growth of the company. It became possible to convert paper, whilst eight embossing machines, two guillotines and several other pieces of equipment such as envelope punches were purchased in the late 1920s and early 30s.

By the start of the Second World War in 1939, GF Smith & Son was making quite a name for itself, not just for its extensive range of beautiful papers but for the extra services it was able

to offer both from the main premises in Hull but also from its sales offices in London.

Unhappily, the Second World War dealt the firm two cruel blows. On the night of 8th May, 1941 in bright moonlight German aircraft dropped 157 tons of high explosive and 20,000 incendiary bombs on the city. Casualties were heavy, and included 116 killed and 160 seriously injured.

Numerous large fires erupted all over Hull, with 150 burning at one time, the largest in the vicinity of the Albert and William Wright Docks and among factories along the river.

Buildings destroyed or damaged included the Prudential Building at the junction of King Edward and Paragon Streets, half of the shops in the city centre, the large Reckitts Works and the Royal Infirmary.

And the premises of GF Smith & Son were bombed flat.

Two nights later the London premises suffered the same fate. The principal assets of the company were reduced to piles of rubble. All stock, records and the majority of the machinery were lost. The only blessing was that no-one from the firm was injured.

Despite GF Smith & Son being reduced to nothing for the second time in 25 years, Mr Thomlinson was not going to be beaten. A private house which was available for rent in Park Avenue, Hull was acquired. Its first floor became the offices and its garage the

warehouse. The house was to be the company's home for six years whilst for a second time the business of GF Smith & Son was rebuilt from scratch.

The company slowly rebuilt and regathered its strength. Despite much of its business being nationwide the firm valued its Hull roots, and in 1945 purchased premises in Lockwood Street, Hull

to replace the temporary Park Avenue house. This ex-ammunition store was bought and refurbished by the firm over the next eighteen months and it began operations there in 1947. These premises remain the company's headquarters today.

In 1948 new premises were also acquired in London. The following years became a period of successful growth for the company. Its workforce grew whilst it continued to develop its reputation as a supplier of special papers to the print community.

Further turmoil however, was to befall the company in the early 1960s. The American owners of GF Smith & Son had themselves recently been the subject of a takeover. The result was that the new, much larger, organisation wanted to concentrate its efforts on growing its home market and therefore decided to divest itself of its UK business.

In 1963 Mr HE Thomlinson together with Mr Cyril Stephenson, Mr Peter Frank and Mr Ted Southern, the company's management team at that time, formulated one of the first management buyouts in the UK paper merchanting trade and bought the company from its American owners. After nearly 50 years the company regained the independence which it proudly protects to this day.

The late 1960s, and particularly the early 1970s, saw a considerable growth in the business. Masterminded by a new Board member, Mr John Alexander, a total revamp of the product range took place: greater emphasis on promoting graphic designers saw the company's reputation in the market increase substantially. A few years later the company successfully diversified into the production of wedding albums and photographic mounts.

As a consequence of such innovation the Lockwood Street premises were expanded substantially in the 1980s and 1990s. By the turn of the Millennium the company was employing 150 people and operating from state of the art narrow-aisle high bay paper warehousing and modern, well-equipped factory facilities at its Lockwood Street and nearby Green Lane sites. These premises continued to be supplemented by a customer service and distribution centre in London.

The workforce is famed for its diligence in 'going the extra mile', whilst the company offers an unrivalled portfolio of the highest quality papers manufactured by the world's leading paper mills - all this is backed by a bespoke service acknowledged amongst other paper suppliers as being 'second to none'.

A team of creative specialists supports each customer's needs in all the company's divisions – working in print, packaging and publishing categories. The firm not only encourages innovation with industry professionals but also with students and schools alike.

Despite its humble origins in Hull over a century ago, through perseverance and the dedication of its loyal workforce, the company now rightfully enjoys the enviable position of being respected market leader in the UK coloured and textured paper market.

Many of the world's leading brands use GF Smith papers and boards for luxury products, marketing materials and packaging. From Rolls Royce's brochures to Paul Smith literature, from Gucci fashion books to the leaders of the hand made card market, GF Smith's papers find themselves adorning millions of creative, inspirational, commercial and personal pieces.

With a worldwide reputation gained, not just for its exquisite product portfolio, but also for its integrity and long standing expertise in the market, the company today is looking forward to its next 100 years in business – though hopefully, in its second century, with a little less rebuilding needed along the way!

Top left, facing page: Smiths premises in the 1960s. **Below left, facing page and this page:** *Interior and exterior views of the GF Smith's Lockwood Street premises, 2008.*

De Smet Rosedowns - Pressed for Time

The story of Rosedowns, one of England's four oldest engineering firms, began in 1777. The founder of Rosedowns was John Todd, a man of great enterprise and endeavour, whose iron foundry and ships chandlery also supplied windmill parts, and, not least cannons. Mr Todd's foundry was situated outside the walls of Hull, towards the developing area of Sculcoates. The road approaching it adopted the name Cannon Street from the activities in the Old Foundry. This is still the company's address today.

During the firm's formative years there were a number of transitory partners. It was known as Todd and Savage, and then became Todd, Fletcher and Co. in 1792. In 1803 Mr Duncan Campbell became the first of a long family line of management.

By the time Todd retired in 1824, the company was known as Todd and Campbell's, and Duncan Campbell became the proprietor. Campbell had been a pupil of the renowned engineer John Smeeton, the constructor of the third lighthouse at Eddystone Rock. It was Campbell who was responsible for developing the seed-crushing side of the business, which went hand in hand with their production of windmill parts.

Duncan Campbell left his land and estates to four trustees and requested that they should carry on the business for the benefit of his family under the style of "Executors of Duncan Campbell, Hull Foundry and Forge." The profits were to be paid to Christiana Rose, his daughter, and were to be used for trading

purposes and to pay off the outstanding mortgage to John Todd. The business carried on under this title until 1851 when the style was changed to "C. Rose, Engineers and Millwrights".

In 1818 Christiana had married widower Captain John Rose, a seafarer. From about 1840 she appears to have been completely dependant upon her own resources for the livelihood of herself and daughter Susannah, now 22,

In 1859, Mrs Rose advertised for a manager. The appointment of Mr James Downs was to lead to the next connection with the Rosedowns name.

Under Downs the business rapidly improved.

Marketing for the firm was worldwide, the company having been responsible for building and installing over 100 double (vertical hydraulic) Anglo-American-type presses between 1861 and 1863.

Susannah married a seed-crusher from Hull, John Thompson, in 1850. They had a son, John junior, in 1853.

Top left: Christina Rose. Top right: The old foundry established in 1777. Above: The company's first Hydraulic Press for expelling oil from Linseed. Above left: James Downs. Far left: Rose and Downs in 1870. Left: John Campbell Thompson.

Downs remained the manager until in 1871, shortly before Mrs Rose died at the age of 78. There were over 200 workmen at her funeral.

Three years later in 1874 the firm became Rose, Downs and Thompson. In accordance with the terms of his grandmother's will John Campbell Thompson became a partner in the firm when he was 21. His exploits abroad gave great stimulus to the company's export business.

Not every foreign contract at the time proved completely successful. When the first hydraulic mill was shipped to China the workforce in Chefoo saw the almost silent rising of the hydraulic rams as the work of demons! They fled in terror, never to return.

Rose, Downs and Thompson became a limited company in 1893. The registered trademark was the now internationally famous 'Rosedowns'. James Downs retired from the company a decade later, having passed the power of attorney onto his eldest son, also called James. Downs senior died in 1904. Then, in 1916, John Campbell Thompson died a bachelor, ending a span of four generations at the helm.

James Downs junior started working for the company in 1873 and was renowned as a man of great culture and wide interests. He began as company secretary, before becoming a director and then chairman, where he remained until his death in 1941.

Charles Downs had started with the company in 1883, and it was he who drove the company through a period of rapid expansion. As managing director in 1903, he greatly extended the premises.

It was at the turn of the 20th Century that the ferro concrete building (the 'white building') was erected. In addition, the company also constructed the bridge on the corner of New Cleveland Street and Holderness Road. As well as the seed-crushing machinery, other products included cranes, Kingston-patent grab dredgers and steam engines.

During the First World War the company produced its fair share of munitions, not least the Constantinesque gear. This synchronised the firing of an aircraft machine gun with the rotation of the propeller, thus avoiding the possibility of shooting oneself down in combat. 1,760 of these gears were made in a single year, along with over 2.5 million shell cases.

During the war, a gun was erected on the roof of the building, ostensibly to scare off enemy aircraft – though it was actually made of wood!

In 1932, a very proud Rosedowns received a letter from the Chief Engineer of the Airship Guarantee Company, a Mr Barnes Wallis, thanking "Chas Downs esq." for the "splendid work" done in making all of the jigs which were used for the detailed assembly of the structure and joints of the R100 Airship. Charles Downs died in 1936 and was succeeded by his son, Leslie Hall Downs. He oversaw further extensions to both the buildings and the plant. It was a transitional period in the production of seed-crushing machinery, as the hydraulic press was being challenged by a new type of press, the screw press.

Production of the screw press gained ground quickly. Their success was such that today's Rosedowns concentrates its

Top left: The works as they appeared in 1914. Centre left: James Downs (younger). Centre right: Charles Downs. Left: The first continuous Screw Press, designed in 1902. Below: A view inside the Light Machine Shop in the 1950s.

manufacturing output on the screw press. It was intrinsically superior then because of its 'continuous' throughput and lower labour costs. The first screw press was made in 1927.

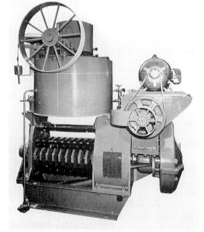

By 1947 over 100 countries would be on Rosedowns list of customers covering oil extraction, from more than 17 different oilseeds. These were processed using solvent extraction as well as screw-pressing.

So it was that the company joined the Power Gas Corporation. A large, chemical engineering plant company was based in Stockton-on-Tees.

The first of the factory whaling ships, the FF Southern Harvester and FF Southern Venturer, were fitted with Rosedowns' fish-processing plant. Driven by a Rover gas turbine engine, a drier and grinder unit was offered with 'no boiler, furnace or electricity required'.

By the 1940s presses were being made in large quantities, and the Maxoil press (which is copied in India today) was even kept in stock by one particular Middle Eastern agent. It was normal for the Maxoil press to be made in batches of 48 or more. In 1943, the price of a press was £485, with electric motor drive.

Rosedowns became part of the Davy-Ashmore group of companies in 1960. This saw a prosperous time for the company. Order books were overflowing.

The company had an excellent social club, situated in its own grounds in Northumberland Avenue. The ladies' tennis team, the cricket team and the bowls team would often travel long distances for inter-company matches, while there were many dance evenings. And all for 2d per week.

Rosedowns again diversified its manufacturing output, as sugar beet was being grown and to meet the growing demand, the company embarked upon the development of the sugar beet press, many of them used in Lincolnshire.

The machine shop was well-equipped, which led to Rosedowns producing large parts such as those for blast furnaces on behalf of the Davy-Ashmore group. Dressing up the castings in the fitting shop was often a punishment for bad lads!

The Davy-Ashmore group changed policy at the dawn of the 1970s, to concentrate on large-scale steel, gas and chemical plants. This led to the acquisition of Rosedowns by Tremletts in 1971, which also procured another Hull business, Richard Sizer.

That year the company received the Queen's Award to Industry for export and achievement.

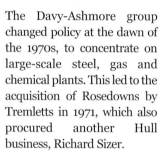

Top left: *Part of the Heavy Machine Shop, 1950s.* ***Above left:*** *A Maxoil press, produced from 1935-1991.* ***Top right:*** *GX Expeller for low pressure rendering.* ***Above:*** *A Lab Press from 1976.* ***Left:*** *The Rose Downs & Thompson works in the 1950s.*

By February 1974, the company was in the more secure hands of Simon Engineering, the largest food-engineering group in the UK.

To celebrate the firm's 200th anniversary in 1977 two cannon barrels were loaned from Hull's museums and gun carriages were made for them. A float appeared at the Lord Mayor's parade and a stand was erected at the Hull show. Most appropriately, 200 model cannons were given as gifts to clients and civil dignitaries.

Late 1988 saw the sale of Rosedowns to De-Smet, with headquarters in Brussels and a well-established leader in the world market.

Screw press design and build was concentrated at Hull, together with an expanding programme of parts production. This investment paid handsome dividends. The company is now enjoying strong export and home market sales, as well as parts supply, and is looking forward to its next 200 years!

*Top: A staff photograph, 1977. **Left:** A Universal 3 TPH Rendering Press produced from 1976 to 1984. **Bottom left:** Rosedowns Mk 3 M 1 TPH Rendering Press, 25 TPD Full Press, 1972 1992. **Below:** The 600 Series 7.0-8.0 TPH Cake Rendering Press, 80 - 100 TPD Full Press, 500 - 600 TPD Pre-Press, 2004-present.*

Donaldson Filters - Ahead of the Rest

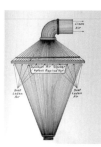

Donaldson is the leading worldwide provider of filtration systems and replacement parts. Founded in 1915, Donaldson is a technology-driven company committed to satisfying customer needs for filtration solutions through innovative research and development. Donaldson serves customers in the industrial and engine markets, including dust collection, power generation, specialty filtration, compressed air purification, off-road equipment, industrial compressors, heavy trucks and light vehicles.

Today the company has annual sales of over $2 billion, more than 12,000 employees, and locations in 35 countries.

Donaldson has been in Europe for more than three decades. Donaldson Europe now has plants in six countries, including Donaldson Filter Components Limited, based on Oslo Road in Hull's Sutton Field Estate.

A 6,000 square metre Hull plant opened in 1980. The facility is a geographically critical manufacturing and distribution operation, which supports Donaldson's industrial air, gas turbine and engine businesses throughout its European markets. Dramatic increases in production volume throughout the 1990s at Hull (and increasing the plant size to 10,000 square metres in 1990) paralleled the whole group's growing air filter business, a growth achieved through a combination of new products, new customers and geographic expansion.

Above left: *Founder, Frank Arthur Donaldson.* **Top:** *Frank Donaldson's stocky frame and ebullient expression were testimony to the comfort of Donaldson Co.'s new development of the late 1920s, a spring tractor seat (inset).* **Above:** *An original patent drawing for one of the first Donaldson filters.* **Right:** *The Twister - a version of Frank Donaldson's first filter.*

Company products contribute significantly towards making the environment cleaner and safer. Those products include air and liquid filters, exhaust and emission control products, in-plant air pollution control systems, air intake systems and exhaust products for industrial gas turbines as well as specialised filters for highly demanding applications such as in aircraft passenger cabins and semiconductor processing.

By the time Robert 'Bob' H Donaldson, the company's 'grand old gentleman', died at the age of 90 in 1978 after 63 years in the business, the company's annual sales had hit $179 million. By the start of the new millennium sales reached $1 billion. The Donaldson story did not start with Bob Donaldson however.

In 1915 Bob's brother Frank, a young man with an outgoing personality and a penchant for large cigars, was a salesman for the Bull Tractor Company of Minneapolis. On a hot day in Utah, Frank arrived at the farm of Hiram Miller: the farmer's new Bull Tractor had stopped in its tracks in the middle of a dusty field. Donaldson had sold the tractor to Miller and was anxious to keep his customer satisfied and so he sent the machine away for a complete overhaul.

Only days after the machine was returned however it broke down again. Donaldson concluded that dirt had accumulated in the intake manifold, killing the engine and wearing down liners, piston rings and other moving parts.

Frank decided to fix the problem himself. Squatting under the hot sun he fashioned a filter made from a wire cage wrapped around a piece of old eiderdown. Mounted on an eight-foot pipe and attached to the engine of the tractor the makeshift filter trapped most of the dirt before it could harm the engine. Without the air cleaner the tractor ground to a halt after two days work - with the filter the tractor tilled the fields day in and day out.

Frank Donaldson felt that he had made a great discovery, and yet Bull Tractors was unimpressed. The company sacked him for not having sufficient confidence in its products!

Back home in St Paul, Minnesota, Frank put his engineering degree to good use. Helped by his tinsmith father, WHL Donaldson, and his brother Bob, Frank set about designing and

*Top: A 1930s company letterhead. **Above left:** Bob Donaldson. **Above:** A shop photograph, Frank Donaldson Sr. pictured second left. **Below:** Donaldson's Pelham plant, 1930s.*

building a completely novel air filter. With tin snippers and soldering irons the three men produced a cone-shaped air filter in which centrifugal force threw out heavier-than-air dirt, which was then collected in a jar.

Frank hit the road with the crude, handmade filters calling on tractor manufacturers. Ironically, one of Frank's first sales would be to the Bull Tractor Company.

In 1917 when the USA entered the First World War: the Donaldson Company landed a lucrative contract to build air cleaners for America's artillery tractors. By war's end in 1918 the Donaldsons were ready to get on with business. Sales grew from $19,554 in 1924 to $204,667 in 1928.

Frank Donaldson's centrifugal air cleaner invention was sold under the trade name of the 'Twister'. In 1920, Donaldson introduced a new filter-type cleaner called the 'Simplex'. It was packed with moss soaked in oil. Dust-laden air entered the Simplex through the oil-soaked moss - a process, which removed almost all the dirt.

The 'Duplex', which combined both types of filter, was patented in 1922. By the close of the 1920s the company was selling 200,000 air filters each year, in addition to exhaust pipes and spring tractor seats. They were also poised to expand dramatically unfortunately, the Wall Street Crash of 1929 put paid to that – and the jobs of three quarters of the company's 40 staff were lost.

For the Donaldson Company however, the economic depression of the 1930s lasted less time than it did for many others. In 1934 the Donaldsons submitted a new 'hat-type' oil washed air cleaner to the Ford Motor Company for testing on its cars. The cleaner, which was mounted directly on a down draft carburettor, surpassed design expectations in three separate areas. Even

under severe road test conditions the air cleaner effectively screened out 99.6 per cent of dirt in the air. In addition the cleaner did not reduce cars' top speed, nor did it increase their

petrol consumption. When news of the cleaner's star performance reached the Donaldson Company there was a great deal of hand shaking and jubilation.

The success of the oil-washed air cleaner with Ford led directly to a sudden and swift recovery for the Donaldson Company. By July 1934, just three months after the company had been reduced to selling some of its patents to raise money, the business was back from the brink.

Donladsons' new air cleaners were being installed on all the cars being manufactured at the Ford Motor Company's, St Paul, Minnesota plant by 1935. Soon shipments were also being sent to Ford plants in Seattle, Omaha, Louisville, Dallas, Kansas City and Detroit. In addition sales were also being made to the famous Caterpillar Tractor Company and John Deere Tractors, as well as to half a dozen other tractor manufacturers throughout the American Midwest. By 1939 sales were approaching $1 million a year as more than 200 Donaldson employees manufactured over 300,000 air cleaners annually, many of which were being exported to Britain, Sweden, New Zealand and Australia. Astonishingly, the Donaldson Company was manufacturing almost 90 per cent of all the air cleaners made for farm and construction equipment in the USA. But soon even more critical demands would be made of Donaldson air filters.

Top left: Original Spanish Moss Air Cleaner and RadialSeal™ Air Cleaner. **Left:** *A Donaldson exhibition stand.* ***Top right:*** *PTFE membrane bondoning in the Membranes Department.* **Above:** *PowerCore filters in round and racetrack configurations, ten times more efficient than average filters.*

During the Second World War, clouds of North African sand chewed up the American tank engines and knocked out as many armoured vehicles as the enemy did at Algeria's Kasserine Pass. The army belatedly called in Donaldson. By revising its 12 inch diameter air cleaners, the one they had been putting on tractors for 25 years, mounting them under armour plate, and installing them on the back of the army's tanks, Donaldson successfully fixed the problem – six decades later Donaldson Ultra-Web filters made in Hull would be helping ensure that British Army vehicles in Iraq and Afghanistan would keep moving however demanding the conditions.

The end of the war would mean leadership changes for the Donaldson Company. In August 1945, the company founder's son, Frank Donaldson junior, was called home from the Navy. The younger Frank was to have been groomed by his father for high office in the company but that would not be possible because Frank Donaldson senior died at the age of 55 just days after his son's return. Fortunately, Frank junior would prove to be as dynamic and entrepreneurial as his father.

With the exception of a short-lived downturn in the early 1980s, company progress would continue unabated.

Most recently has come the PowerCore range of filters developed by Donaldson in 2002, the second generation of which, PowerCore G2, has been produced in Hull since 2008. PowerCore filters using patented Ultra-Web nanofibre filtration are up to ten times more compact and efficient than standard pleated cellulose filters, and are now being fitted by JCB to the world's fastest diesel engines.

Today, the legacy of that inventive young salesman Frank Donaldson, who devised his first air filter under a blazing summer sun in 1915 from chicken wire and an old eiderdown, is a staggeringly successful multi-national business. Millions of people now benefit from the work that goes on at Donaldson, in particular in Hull where 330 employees achieve an annual turnover of more than 63 million Euros. Donaldson definitely made a sound decision coming to East Yorkshire.

Top left: *Members of staff recieving their NVQ certificates as Donaldson train all employees to a minimum NVQ2 level in continuous improvement techniques.* ***Above and left:*** *Donaldson Spiracle™ crankcase filtration system. The numbered image shows the unique two stage filtration system. Number 1 is the first filter stage, filter media in the centre grid employs high velocity impaction technology for coalescing airborne hydrocarbon vapour, soot and engine oil contaminates. This stage provides an average efficiency in excess of 50%. Numbered 2, the second stage uses low velocity diffusion technology for extremely high efficiency, resulting in over 90% total filtration efficiency. Both filter stages are integrated into a single, replaceable filter cartridge.* ***Left:*** *Celebrating 25 years of production at the Hull operation. Back row from left to right: Robin Atkinson Production Manager, Ian Jowett Finance Director, Marc Deschilder Plant Manager, Charlie McMurray SVP, Vince Milestone PPC manager, Jacques Van Peteghem Bruge Plant Manager, Peter Halstead UK Sales Manager. Front row from left to right: Henk Houf Germany Plant Manager, Steve Leverenz Global Logistics Director, Lowell Schwab SVP, Ian Metcalfe Quality Manager.* ***Below:*** *The company premises in Hull, Oslo Rd, Sutton Fields Estate.*

Ideal Standard; Moving Successfully Through its Second Century

Acentury ago standards of domestic sanitation were not what they are today. But things had been improving, if slowly, for a very long time: Sir John Harrison built the world's first flushing toilet for Queen Elizabeth in 1589. The first public loo opened in London in 1858: it would be followed by many thousands of others. Some were veritable palaces celebrating the art and skills of the plumber and the potter, and in turn helped create a demand amongst the public for better facilities in their own homes.

Today every home has a bathroom: sometimes more than one. But most readers will recall the days when some houses had no bathroom and many had only an outside loo. One of the greatest pleasures today, for those who recall those times, is simply taking a warm bath on a freezing cold winter's evening, and luxuriating in the comfort of a centrally heated bathroom. The good old days weren't always so good in a chilly December!

Top left: The proposed factory site in 1905. Below: The cornerstone laying ceremony on May 31, 1906 attended by Mayor Larard and his councillors. Above right: A Rococo dining room radiator, complete with food warmer. Right: The company's first Managing Director Henry Downe (track-level, second right) stands - with some pride - in front of National's new switch engine, which would ferry materials to the site.

Much of the impetus for that change in our living standards over the course of the 20th century is down to work done in Hull, by what is now the Ideal Standard company and its employees at its factory in National Avenue.

Ideal Standard's history in Hull goes back to 1906 when the American-owned National Radiator Company set up a new factory employing 800 people to make its Ideal brand of central heating radiators.

On 21st December 1906 the furnace was lit and soon afterwards the first cast iron radiator to be made in Britain emerged from its still-glowing mould.

Demand for the new and previously all but unheard of central heating radiators was huge, and by 1910 there were 1,000 men on site. When war broke out in 1914 however, a large part of the works was turned over to producing munitions. By the end of 1915 the factory was run almost exclusively by women when all the men left to join the armed forces.

Following the ending of the Great War in 1918 a wider variety of products were manufactured including cast iron cookers and domestic boilers.

Meanwhile, far from Hull, merger talks were going on between National Radiator's owners, the American Radiator Company, and the USA's largest manufacture of cast iron bath tubs and plumbing supplies - the

Standard Sanitary Manufacturing Company. Eventually, on 26 March 1929, a new consolidated business came into being: the American Radiator and Standard Sanitary Corporation.

In 1936 the British end of the new business had changed its name to Ideal Boilers & Radiators Limited, but even by this time cast iron enamelled baths were also being made in Hull - and a vitreous china factory was in the process of being built, the first ever in Britain outside of the Potteries. Soon 500 pottery pieces a day were being produced in Hull and a second kiln was under construction.

Pottery and kilns are pretty fragile things, yet despite intensive German bombing during the Second World War no German bombs landed on what was by now a 54 acre site - the only wartime damage being done by a stray shell from our own side!

Though the Hull factory may have escaped damage neither the rest of Hull nor the rest of the country was so lucky: a massive rebuilding programme began after war ended. Houses could not be built fast enough, and with the demand for new houses grew the

demand for boilers and baths. Even operating at full capacity the Ideal factory could not keep up.

Ideal had little choice but to restrict sales and carefully ration its customers.

In 1950 a completely new production line was opened that could make 100,000 cast iron baths a year - enough to form an unbroken line of baths all the way from Hull to Birmingham. Two years later a third kiln was lit in the company's pottery taking capacity up from 150,000 pieces of vitreous china per annum to 250,000. Not long afterwards new techniques reducing firing times boosted the pottery's output to a massive 400,000 pieces a year - a figure approaching one piece per minute every minute of the year. By 1955 the Ideal pottery was producing four times as much as it had just a few years previously.

In the meantime demand for cast iron radiators was declining in the face of competition from pressed steel radiators. Not even massive, and ultimately wasted investment in new production techniques could save the situation.

Top left: The Ideal road show, displaying Ideal's products in a domestic setting. Top right: Advertising for Ideal Britannia Boilers. Above left: The Standard Ejecto syphon action washdown closet. Above: The Hull plant, circa 1930s.

In the mid 1950s the last radiator left the foundry.

Though all may have been doom and gloom in the foundry elsewhere the future was rosy. In 1961 the company changed its name again: this time to Ideal Standard, uniting by name two well - known brands that had already long been part of one company. By 1963 production in the pottery was up to 2,000 pieces a day and a research and development department, devoted to bathroom products, was working full time on new product lines.

Henry Ford had once famously said that car buyers could have any colour they wanted so long as it was black: and bathroom manufacturers had offered any colour so long as it was white. Now home owners were demanding a choice in the price and style of their bathroom fixtures as in everything else. Competition for the increasing disposable income came from cars, TVs and foreign holidays as much as from rival bathroom manufacturers. Ideal Standard had to react, making its range more contemporary. Bathrooms were still expensive, but the opportunity was arising to produce

designs so eye catching that they drew the passer-by into shops simply on the strength of seeing the new designs in the shop window.

Ideal Standard responded to the challenge by producing its 'Kingston' range which would be its flagship for a decade, as well as 'Trimline', the first lightweight vitreous china suite to be made in Britain.

In 1964 Ideal Standard updated the choice of colours in its bathroom ranges: as well as white customers could now have sky blue or turquoise. Step by step the industry was becoming more customer oriented, and discovering how to rejuvenate the appeal of their products through design.

The only thing that is permanent is change. Nowhere has that old proverb been more true than at Ideal Standard, not least in the 1970s. Cast iron was by this stage yesterday's material. Acrylic in all its new colours had usurped iron as an affordable, fashionable material for moulding baths. New models could now be introduced with much lower tooling costs. Idea Standard ended the production of cast iron baths in 1970.

Top left: Radio and Television star Terry Thomas drops in on an Ideal exhibition stand at the time of the Festival of Britain, 1951. *Top right:* A young Duke of Edinburgh visits the plant in December 1948. *Above:* One of the company's Sottini collection luxury basin units, 1996. *Left:* Open day at Ideal Standard.

The company was however still the market leader in cast iron boilers, but the loss of first radiators and then baths meant that the Ideal Standard foundry was facing a bleak future. Cast iron was from another age: although produced with pride by generations of foundrymen at Hull it was a hot laborious and dirty endeavour compared to the quick clean, automated processing of plastic or steel. The foundry was sold to the Stelrad Group in September 1976, a company which would continue to make the Ideal brand boiler.

The freeing up of space would allow a new office block to be built on National Avenue on part of the original cast iron bath plant, but more importantly, allow the company to focus exclusively on what it did best: to be a designer-led manufacturer offering exciting bathroom products or as some put it 'practical sculpture'.

In the decades since 1976 Ideal Standard would more than live up to the high expectations of its managers, employees and shareholders producing range after range of memorable and high quality bathroom furniture which would be increasingly popular with the public.

The National Radiator Company, Ideal Standard's founder, first opened offices in Britain in 1896. In 1996 Ideal Standard was able to celebrate its centenary, not only by reflecting on 100 years of remarkable progress, but also by launching yet another new designer bathroom range, the much copied, though never bettered, Kyomi suite.

In 1999 the company purchased is greatest rival, and the best known bathroom brand Armitage Shanks. These days 90% of products manufactured in Ideal Standard's four factories within the UK are sold within the UK.

Since arriving in Hull in 1906 much has changed in the world as well as in the firm: and though Ideal Standard may no longer have a reputation for designs in cast iron it has certainly maintained its cast iron reputation for design. Today Ideal Standard continues to work with renowned designers, the latest range being designed by UK designer Jasper Morrison.

There can surely be no doubt that the 21st century will see Ideal Standard continue to maintain its position as one of the brightest jewels in the city of Hull's industrial crown.

Above: The Berger Colouring Our Lives Award for fashion in the home, won in 1988. **Below left:** *Part of Ideal's Jasper Morrison bathroom range.* **Below:** *Staff pictured at Brocket Hall.*

Fishgate - Hull Fish Auction - A Vital Link

Fishgate - Hull Fish Auction Ltd - is the centre point of Hull's seafood industry bringing fresh fish from the northern seas off Iceland, Faroe and Norway. Built in 2000 today's market is a state-of-the-art fish auction facility with temperature control and computer-tracking of the products from reception to dispatch. All fish is graded to a high level of size-grade accuracy and put on display in plastic boxes of a 40kg nominal weight, with each box labelled to the precise weight, species and origin.

The auction takes place at 7 each morning, and buyers either attend the auction or bid online. Immediate dispatch can be made to locations throughout Western Europe.

It was in the late 1990s that Hull decided that it would build a market that was everything that the food industry was demanding in food safety, quality and traceability.

Visitors from all over the world have now seen what Hull can offer. The market has put down a benchmark that has become a standard for marketing what is one of the finest nutritious foods that nature can provide.

It was not until 1840 that Hull began to emerge as an important fishing port. The catalyst for this development was the arrival of the railways. The railway could distribute fresh fish to the inland towns and cities where

*Left: A barrow boy in the late 1940s. **Below:** St Andrews Dock in the 1960s, opened in 1883.*

An ice factory opened on the south side of St. Andrews Dock in 1891. Until then ice had been shipped from Norway and kept in underground bunkers insulated from strong sunlight and warm air.

The St Andrews Dock Extension was opened in 1895 to cater for the continued growth in fleet size and volume. Hull by now had three quarters of a mile of dockside for unloading fish. The following year, however, a dam at the west end of the extension gave way and a great surge of water flooded into the dock; the flood wrecked several ships, but remarkably there were no fatalities. The sight must have been spectacular if somewhat terrifying for those who witnessed the event.

the growing workforce and their families needed cheap food. Until that time fresh fish rarely travelled more than a few miles from the coast.

In 1869 West Dock (now Albert Dock) was built and was used as a fish dock. By then some 500 trawling smacks were using the port.

St. Andrews Dock was opened 1883 specifically to serve the fishing industry which was growing apace. The dock's location was where PC World and Currys are now to be found. Hull's first steam trawler, the Magenta, started to operate from the port about this time. Steam rapidly replaced sail power, and by 1900 there were very few of the old sailing trawlers left.

A fishmeal plant had opened on the South side in 1890. The raw material came from unsold fish which in those days was a significant amount. The use of fish offal for fishmeal came much later, as at this time all fish from Hull was dispatched in whole form for inland fishmongers to fillet and process for their customers.

In 1899 a 'cod farm' was established at the west end of the extension for drying cod that could not be sold as iced fish.

Top left: Bobbers unloading a trawler into ten stone wooden kits, later replaced in the 1950s by aluminium kits (see picture below). Below left: Buyers cluster around the auction at sale time. Below: A buyer surveys the fish for sale before the auction.

Unlike fresh fish the dried cod had a shelf life of many months and were mainly exported abroad since there was little market for them in the UK.

Up to the start of the First World War in 1914 much of the North Sea (which until then was often still called the German Sea) Hull fleet was engaged in 'fleeting'. The trawlers joined a fleet of similar vessels under the command of an 'admiral' who directed trawling operations. Each morning the combined catch was put aboard a fleet cutter that took the fresh fish direct to Billingsgate fish market in London. The vessels only came home when they ran short of coal. It was a remarkable industrial process but one of great danger to the crews.

Though fishing continued through the war years of 1914-18 most of the fleet saw war service of one kind or another. With peace, however, came a time of great prosperity for Hull. In the 1920s came an expansion of distant water operations to Iceland, Bear Island, the Norway Coast, and the Barents Sea. New bigger trawlers were built.

It was in the 1920s that filleting on the dockside took place for the first time. Until then all fish was sent whole to the inland

markets, or direct to fishmongers, who prepared the fish for their own customers. Dockside filleting eventually led to the huge processing industry of the 1930s and the immediate post war period of the late 1940s.

By 1922 fish landings in Hull had reached 90,000 tons per year. With that sort of volume a new market building was needed, and by the late 1920s construction was well underway. Unhappily in 1929 Hull's new market building caught fire and was totally destroyed before it had even opened. It would be the biggest fire in Hull until the Second World War.

Despite such setbacks, landings grew to an astonishing 320,000 tons by 1936. The fish had a market value of £4.6m (in 2007 by contrast Fishgate sold over 14,000 tons for around £22m). In those years there were some 200 distant water trawlers regularly operating out of Hull. This truly made Hull the greatest fishing port in the world.

During the Second World War most of the Hull trawler fleet was requisitioned for service in the Royal Navy. A number of older vessels, however, transferred to Fleetwood on the safer west coast. A result Hull virtually wound down to become a very minor fishing port for the duration of the war.

Happily the outbreak of peace in 1945 saw the start of a post-war boom, with the fleet returning and being built up again. Landings were up, but they would never reach the record figure achieved in 1936.

During the 1960s freezing at sea became an established part of the fishing industry with Hull playing a major part in its introduction. This resulted in major changes to the way fish was marketed in the UK and elsewhere.

Yet troubles were never far away. Between 1959 and 1976 there were numerous disputes and three cod wars with Iceland, together with the progressive expansion of fishery limits in all countries to 200 miles. These events led to the demise of the distant water fleets and a progressive decline of Hull as a fishing port. The city, however, retained an active fish processing industry.

In 1975 St Andrews Dock was closed and filled in. The site became the retail park it is today. The fish industry moved back to Albert Dock after 92 years and the fish auction market was established there in three cargo warehouses on the south side.

More than two decades later, in 1997, a working group was established to decide on the future of fish marketing in Hull. Three choices were available – to do nothing except to remain in the warehouses in Albert Dock, to improve the warehouses with insulation and refrigeration, or build an entirely new market alongside the William Wright Dock (which had joined with the Albert Dock in 1910).

The decision was taken was to build anew. It was a bold venture, but one which had universal support from the industry in Hull. The feeling was that Hull had to move with the times and build the best market in the country, and become a shop window for Icelandic fish which was by then the dominant source of supply. That brave decision eventually resulted in Fishgate which opened its doors in 2001.

By 2002 Fishgate had achieved all its creators' ambitions, not least securing the EFSIS Award - now the British Retail Consortium Global Standard - for good practice.

Today the company maintains the high food safety standards demanded by the BRC Global Standard through EFSIS. These are audited annually and the company monitors its own performance and quality control regularly. It has a highly skilled workforce and HACCP procedures are in place.

Though Hull may have virtually ceased to operate as a fishing port it possesses not only one of the finest markets in the world but remains a vital link in the global fish supply chain, utilising knowledge and skills built up over 170 years.

Facing page: Various views inside the temperature controlled auction hall at Fishgate. **Left and above:** Electronic auction theatre at Fishgate. **Below:** An ariel view of Fishgate in 2002.

Hull Truck Theatre - The Play's the Thing

Television and the cinema may be all right for some; but for those in the know, nothing can compete with the experience of live theatre. Watching a real performance by real live actors whilst sitting amongst an enraptured audience has a quality which simply cannot be replicated on either the small or large screen. For a child a first visit to a live theatre is an unforgettable experience, a memory which will last a lifetime.

Though the citizens of many towns and cities have far too infrequent opportunities to experience live performances for themselves, Hull is remarkably lucky.

Established in 1971 Hull Truck is one of just six producing theatres in the Yorkshire region. From 1983 it provided a vast range of activities from its very modest, former church hall, Spring Street home. Over the years the company has carved out an outstanding reputation as one of the innovators and forerunners of British theatre.

In just one recent year a phenomenal twelve plays were produced by Hull Truck, delivered by seven different writers, including three new commissions and one adaptation. Three plays went on tour nationally, whilst at home in Hull 244 performances of Hull Truck productions were performed in front of 52,000 people. Local knowledge and personal resonance with the growing audience has been a defining strength of Hull Truck with many productions set within the city and surrounding region.

Completing construction of a new state-of-the-art building in 2008 the company's enduring passion, vision and unique brand has continued to flourish.

Founding Director Mike Bradwell worked with the Theatre company between 1971 and 1982. He had decided to form a new theatre company in 1971 and placed an advert in Time Out, but half the original company dropped out when they discovered they were to be taken north to work in Hull!

The acting company acquired its name after touring and performing out of the back of a truck from 1971 to 1983.

In 1972, after three months of rehearsing through improvisation around a paraffin stove in a cold damp rented house in Coltman Street in Hull, the company's first play *The Children Of The Lost Planet* opened at the Gulbenkian Studio Theatre, Newcastle upon Tyne on 10th March. Although well received, it resulted in

Following the first production of *Bouncers* at Hull Truck in 1984, Hull Truck released the *'Bouncers Rap'* was released as a single which led to an appearance on The Tube. *Bouncers* has won seven Los Angles Drama Critics Circle Awards.

That year audience figures were recorded as 40,000.

John Godber's famous comedy, *Teechers*, was first performed at Hull Truck in 1987 and would eventually also be part of the final season's line-up at the Spring Street venue in Autumn 2008.

The company's 15th anniversary in 1986 was marked by LWT's The South Bank Show devoting a whole programme telling the Hull Truck Story.

Meanwhile plans were being drawn up for Hull Truck's new 440-seat theatre in the centre of Hull, plans which would gain approval in 1987.

In 1988, Hull Truck marked an anniversary for the city, the 25th anniversary of The Beatles concert at Hull's Regal Cinema, with the play *A Hard Days Night* by Frederick Harrison.

During the final year of the 1980s, over a quarter of a million people saw Hull Truck on tour.

few bookings. The company next devised *The Land of Woo*, the first of several children's shows, which was performed in a nun's garage at an orphanage.

The adult-only show, *The Mackintosh Cabaret*, was banned in Hull in 1973 because of its 'naughtiness'.

In 1974, the company was commissioned to produce a play for BBC's first Second City series. *The Writing On The Wall* was screened on BBC TV in 1975. This was the beginning of a long-standing relationship between Hull Truck and the BBC.

Hull Truck is a non-profit organisation, and became a charity in June 1975.

The following year was a turning point in the company's financial fortunes, with the first substantial grant from the Arts Council of Great Britain.

Hull Truck Theatre finally opened a base venue in 1983, named Spring Street Theatre. It opened with *The Adventures Of Jasper Ridley* by Nigel Williams on 4th April with a capacity audience of 200.

In its first full financial year Hull Truck had 30,000 customers through its Spring Street doors.

Joint Artistic Director, and BAFTA award-winning playwright, John Godber had joined the company in 1983 and has continued to push the boundaries of contemporary theatre ever since.

September in the Rain, John Godber's first play at Hull Truck Theatre, toured in 1984. In the same year *Up 'n' Under* won an Edinburgh Fringe First, and the Laurence Olivier Comedy of the Year Award, the latter after only six performances in the West End.

Left: Hull Truck Theatre's former Spring Street premises. Above: Out on the road with Hull Truck Theatre. Below: BAFTA award-winning playwright, John Godber.

Photographer: Adrian Gatie

Romeo and Juliet toured nationally in 1990, featuring Roland Gift, lead singer with Fine Young Cannibals, before performing at the International Theatre Festival at the University of New York.

In April 1994 the Spring Street venue received a refurbishment increasing its capacity to 293 seats. The name was changed from Hull Truck Spring Street Theatre to Hull Truck Theatre. True to its remit of innovation and commitment to new writing, the season began with the world premiere of John Godber's *Passion Killers*.

A special gala performance of *It Started With A Kiss* in aid of Hull Truck's fundraising appeal took place in 1997.

In 1999, the hard work of the Hull Truck team was recognised at the prestigious annual Chartered Institute of Marketing Awards, where the theatre was delighted to win first and second prize in its category. Hull Truck was again acknowledged in 2000, being the runners up for the award in marketing excellence.

John Godber's talent was further endorsed in the Autumn of 1999, when his cult classic, *Bouncers*, was ranked by the National Theatre's NT2000 poll as one of the greatest plays of the century.

The Hull Truck Youth Theatre was set up in 1999, with a resident Education department running workshops and working within the community. The first Youth Theatre performance was *Transformations*, written and directed by Hull Truck's then Education Officer Catherine MacPherson.

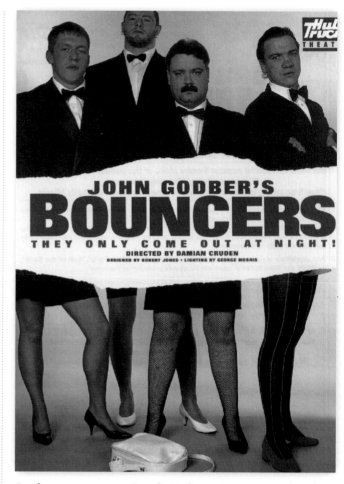

In the 21st century, Gareth Tudor Price was appointed as Associate Director in 2002 and then Joint Artistic Director in 2007.

Artistic impression courtesy Hayes Davidson

The theatre was rewarded for its Arts and Business partnership, with Smith & Nephew and the Children's University, winning the Arts and Business regional award for partnership excellence, in 2003. *Truck Tales*, Hull Truck's Saturday afternoon storytelling performances for children was launched in 2003.

In 2004, Alan Plater's *Confessions Of A City Supporter* was premiered celebrating Hull City's centenary, the new KC Stadium and the football club's promotion to Division One. During the year 60,000 people attended performances by the company.

Hull Truck launched its online ticketing service in November 2006. That same month work got underway on the Ferensway site of the company's brand new state-of-the-art venue.

To crown the year, Hull Truck won the prestigious Office Angels Office of The Year Award in 2006.

Sully, a dramatisation of the life of rugby hero Clive Sullivan was performed at Hull Truck in 2006 and 2007. The play was written by local playwright and journalist Dave Windass.

Another play by the renowned Richard Bean, *Up On Roof* - the gritty smash-hit drama about the Hull Prison riot of 1976 - premiered to high critical acclaim in 2006.

Following an invitation from Right Hon. John Prescott MP, the Youth Theatre performed *Slavers*, commissioned to mark the Wilberforce 2007 bi-centenary, at the Houses of Parliament as part of the British Council slavery debate, becoming the first ever theatre company in history to stage a play at Westminster.

The construction of Hull Truck's new state-of-the-art building was due for completion in Autumn 2008, with the first performances in the new venue scheduled for Spring 2009.

According to Joint Artistic Director John Godber: 'The church hall which we have called home since 1983 was no longer big enough for the company's creative ambition. We needed a building which reflects our reputation and provides the region with a state-of-the-art theatre'.

Hull Truck Theatre's new building has been sited prominently on Ferensway. It has been carefully designed by Wright and Wright to retain the intimate feel of the Spring Street venue, whilst providing many additional facilities beyond the 440 seat main auditorium.

Those new facilities include amenities for educational work enabling Hull Truck's Education Department to play an increasingly important role in the local community.

A 134 seat studio theatre offers a platform for new writers and experimental work as well as being a resource for community and educational groups. The venue also offers improved corporate hospitality facilities for conferences, meetings and presentations.

Top left: *Bouncers, ranked by the National Theatre's NT2000 poll as one of the greatest plays of the century.*
Left and above: *Part of the new 440 seat auditorium at Hull Truck Theatre's new state-of-the-art building, pictured above.*

From Robinson & Sawdon to R&S

Today R&S is one of the major building companies in the Yorkshire and Humber region. Formed in 1921 as Robinson & Sawdon Ltd the firm has grown in size and stature to become an established and respected contractor throughout the north.

Personal attention to every detail, and a guaranteed first class building service, has been the trademark of Robinson and Sawdon Ltd. The company has played a significant role in shaping today's East Yorkshire and has been responsible for creating many of the familiar landmarks in and around Hull.

Robinson and Sawdon Ltd's story actually begins in December of 1915, on the edge of the Canadian prairies 1,000 miles west of Montreal, with a knock on the front door of Fred Robinson's  home in Port Arthur. There were several feet of snow on the ground and Fred, a bricklayer from Hull who had emigrated four years earlier, was surprised to hear the stranger say "My name is Arthur Sawdon. I am a bricklayer from Hull and have just arrived in this one horse town. Can you put me up for the night until I find lodgings?"

Fred Robinson returned to Hull in 1921 to establish his own business. His first commission was to build a bungalow at the corner of Cottingham Road and Ferens Avenue for a Mr Lazenby, a director of Needler's, the chocolate manufacturers.

The following year Fred answered a knock on the door of his home in King's Gardens to be greeted by Arthur Sawdon, "We met in the mid-west of Canada in 1915" he said "I understand that you have started on your own. Do you want a partner?" The two men worked seven days a week, aiming to build a business with a reputation for good work, personal service, fast completion and highly competitive pricing. Their efforts paid off, and by the mid twenties, Fred Robinson and Arthur Sawdon formed a limited company and began working for local authorities as well as building private dwellings.

Notable projects were three housing estates at Beverley - the Swinemoor Lane, Cherry Tree and Admiral Walker estates. Growth continued into the 1930s, with more housing estate

Top: The Robsaw Royals baseball team, Denis Robinson is standing second from the right. *Left:* An artists impression of the Porter Street flats built by Robinson & Sawdon. ***Bottom left:*** The Half Moon at Elloughton which was completed in 1939. ***Below:*** Tivoli House on Paragon Street completed in 1960.

contracts, industrial work and several school building programmes, including Fifth Avenue School, two schools in Endyke Lane, one in Hill Road as well as the Sacred Heart Catholic School. This was followed by some church work; they also built some four and five storey blocks of flats in Porter Street.

Richard (Dick) Sawdon and Denis Robinson, sons of the founders, joined the company during the 1930s having successfully completed building apprenticeships and becoming Fellows of the Institute of Building. With the outbreak of the Second World War Denis joined the armed forces and Richard worked for the Royal Engineers on coastal defence projects.

Sadly Arthur Sawdon died suddenly in May 1940 at the age of just 50. Fred Robinson steered the company through the war years, building large air-raid shelters for industry and carrying out war damage repair work. They were also main sub-contractor to the Admiralty, working round the clock replacing fire-bricks in the boilers of Royal Navy and Merchant Navy vessels.

Dick and Denis resumed working for the company after the war and gradually Fred Robinson handed over full control of the company to them. Robinson and Sawdon Ltd. played a major role in creating a complete city from the badly bombed, rubble-strewn streets of Hull.

Over the next three decades the company undertook a wide variety of projects including, roads and sewers, industrial units, processing mills, warehouses, engineering works, fish processing factories, houses, law courts, city centre office blocks, swimming pools, gas terminal works, public houses and fifteen schools. The company repeatedly demonstrated its versatility and flexible policy of tackling any type of building work no matter how large or small.

Today, R&S is under the new ownership of James Deacon, who purchased the company in 2006. Based at Alexandra House on English Street, R&S has an impressive reputation for reliability and technical expertise and for delivering the same high standard of service first set by its founders. Standards that have been recognised in the construction industry by numerous prestigious awards. Recognising best practice in the construction industry, R&S was named the best company in the region for 'Leadership and People Development' and saw Managing Director James Deacon pick up the prestigious 'Outstanding Achievement Award'. The Workforce Development award was awarded to R&S in recognition of the commitment the company gives to each and every member of staff in the organisation. R&S have also been recognised once again as a key player in the region's construction industry by being shortlisted for Yorkshire Post Excellence in Business Awards in 2008.

R&S are looking forward to the future with optimism, continuing the same high standard of workmanship that has won the company many architectural awards and which has always been the company's firm foundation.

Top left, top right and above left: *A selection of recent projects undertaken by Robinson & Sawdon: Trade Centre complete for Hull & Humber (top left), Brynmor Jones Library at Hull University (top right) and Cherub Nursery Child Care Facility (above left).* ***Below:*** *Managing Director, James Deacon (right) receives yet another award at the Hull Daily Mail Business Awards, 2007.*

F. R. Scott - Ironmongery in the Blood

From its 30,000 square feet of warehousing, conveniently located in Canning Street in the centre of Hull, F.R. Scott Ltd offers its customers a vast choice of fasteners, ironmongery and tools from stock. With 20,000 items available 'off the shelf' almost any requirement can be satisfied immediately.

The firm was founded by the late Fred R. Scott in 1943. Today this family firm continues to flourish.

Fred Scott began his working life as an apprentice for his uncle, Fred Searby, Ironmonger of Great Union Street, Hull. Fred later joined the firm of F & T Ross Ltd in Myton Street, where he eventually worked his way up to become General Manager and Director.

He continued to manage the ironmongery side of the business in Great Union Street until 1942, when the premises were destroyed and the entire stock lost during the blitz.

Nothing was left but an unquenchable spirit. Fred Scott immediately set about the salvage of the business and formed F.R. Scott Ltd on Castle Street, which included F. & T. Ross Ltd and Fred Searby Ironmonger, and numbered some of his staff as its shareholders. The company was incorporated on 13th October, 1945.

Over the years the company has changed greatly to meet its customers' needs. The days are now long gone when horseshoes, oil lamps and cast iron cooking pots were supplied from stock; now however, F.R. Scott Ltd

carries what is almost certainly the most extensive range of bolts and nuts in East Yorkshire, together with a vast range of ironmongery and tools. Allied to this Aladdin's cave of ironmongery is Scott's heating department which will execute all types of industrial heating and pipe-work

installations. The heating department will also undertake routine maintenance of industrial and commercial systems - a twenty-four hour call out service being available if problems arise.

In September 1965, company founder Fred Scott died at the age of 75. He was a Freeman of the City of London and was sorely missed in local circles. His son Peter Scott, who had

Top left: Founder, Fred R. Scott. **Below left:** F.R. Scott's old Castle Street premises. **Above:** The shop on Paragon Square in the early 1960s. **Below:** Staff all ready to embark on a works outing in 1945.

interest within the business. Today Robert Scott is Managing Director, and his father Peter is Chairman.

Recent times have seen more change. The year 2008 had already brought great changes to F. R. Scott Ltd.: being surrounded by the new St. Stephen's Shopping Centre encouraged the company to double the size of the shop area, which in turn has enabled the firm to properly display its ever-expanding range of architectural ironmongery.

worked with his father for 20 years succeeded him as Managing Director and continued the expansion of the business.

It became apparent to Peter in the late 1970s that more space was required to cope with customer demand, and in

Today the company foresees the ironmongery side of the business expanding in the coming years: its fully qualified Registered Architectural Ironmongers can usually find an answer to even the most difficult questions posed by customers.

F. R. Scott Ltd. was awarded the 'Guildmark' in 2008 by 'GAI' the Guild of Architectural Ironmongers, amply illustrating the company's commitment to providing a full professional service.

Scott's is a business based on more than sixty years experience: with its large premises, dedicated staff, caring management and renowned customer service, F.R. Scott Ltd is certainly a firm with lots to look forward to.

1982 new premises were acquired in Canning Street, with customer-car parking for over fifty cars.

The range of stock is so diverse that a customer was once heard to say "If Scott's haven't got it -you don't need it".

The secret of Scott's continuing success is that meeting customers' needs is of paramount importance to the firm. The service given by the counter staff, sales office and skilled heating engineers all helps to make it possible to meet those needs. Nothing is too much trouble, no sale too small, and the fleet of vans delivering, throughout the county and beyond ensure that the customers' requirements are met promptly.

*Top left: A company van in the 1950s. **Above left:** Scott's Portland Place works in 1979. **Above:** An example of the vast selection of products available at Scott's. **Below:** F.R. Scott's Canning Street premises, 2008.*

None of this would be possible without the dedication and experience of the firm's fifty staff, some of whom have been at Scott's for over 40 years.

In 1981, Peter's son Robert, grandson of the founder, joined the company, so continuing the family

Henry Hird Ltd - the Jewel of Hessle Road

Henry Hird Ltd Jewellers in Hull's Hessle Road has been in business since the 1850s. During that time members of just two families have run the firm. Inevitably the traditional jeweller has become a very well known and respected business.

Today Henry Hird Ltd is almost certainly the oldest jewellers in Hull, and it remains the place to visit for those who want good old-fashioned service from people who care. From ready-made jewellery to customers' own designs, Henry Hird's provides the full service. Everyone on Hessle Road got their wedding rings from Henry Hird or 'Hy Hird' as it said over the door – a name that puzzled generations of children. Today a great many people from the local area and far beyond still get their wedding rings, and every other kind of jewellery from Hird's.

Henry Hird's was long known as the trawlerman's jeweller. Men flush with money from the sea would come home and often spend their wages there (or at least what they had left from being

in Raynor's the pub further along the road) and buy their wives a trinket.

The clock outside the firm's premises at 270 Hessle Road readily identifies the business which has been trading at that address since it moved there at the turn of the 20th century.

The firm's founder, the original Henry Hird, had opened premises in Cumberland Street in 1852.

It was a good time to start a new luxury business. By then, the fishing industry was taking off in Hull. Trade and industry were boosted by the arrival of the rail link with Leeds in 1840. In the 1840s, the 'silver pits' – a very fish-rich part of the North Sea –

led to fishermen from Devon and Kent migrating to the Humber, at first seasonally and then permanently. The introduction in the late 19th century of new fishing methods – the "trawl" – and of steam powered trawlers, meant that Hull fishermen fished as far a field as Iceland and the White Sea and made good wages for the times. By then it was the founder's son, Henry Cook Hird, who was in charge when the jewellery business moved to Hessle Road. When his father died in 1921 Henry Cook Hird took over. And he recruited to the staff Phyllis Price who would work for the firm for the next 69 years.

Phyllis Price's son David Whincup joined the firm in 1956 after doing his National Service in the Army. Post war austerity meant few people were buying luxuries, but the demand for engagement rings and wedding rings had never been higher.

David Whincup worked at Hird's for the next forty years. Following his death the business passed into the ownership of his sister Yvonne Smith. When the business passed to Yvonne Smith she was then 63 and working as a nurse. Though only a few weeks from retirement she had no qualms about taking on the challenge. Yvonne had been a regular visitor to the shop since her childhood when she could recall having desperately

wished to be taller so she could see over the counter and look at the jewellery for sale.

The highlight of the shop's past was those days when trawler men came in. "They would have a three day break from the sea and bring their wives and girlfriends in to treat them" Yvonne would recall. When houses were demolished in the area 11,000 people were relocated and it was thought that the business might suffer badly, yet such was the firm's reputation that loyal customers still come from far and wide

Today framed pictures of the previous owners hang in the shop, a reminder of the long and proud history of the firm.

Philip Smith has been in charge since 2005. He started to help

out in the shop aged just ten. When David Whincup became ill Philip got a full time job there aged 21 and thus became the 6th owner of Henry Hird Ltd jewellers. Philip Smith runs the business today with long standing members of the staff Philip Gray and Sandra Cole.

Facing page: Henry Hird, Hessle Road, in 1950s (bottom) and 1964 (top). Above left: David Whincup. Above: Yvonne Smith. Left: Philip Smith, owner of Henry Hird Ltd.

Reckitt Benckiser - Two Centuries of Business

Today, still located in Dansom Lane, the origins of the international company, Reckitt Benckiser (previously Reckitt and Colman) can be traced back to the early 19th century when Isaac Reckitt, Jeremiah Colman and Johann A Benckiser began their separate businesses.

Isaac Reckitt had a mill in Boston, Lincolnshire, as early as 1819. His business in Hull began with a starch factory in Dansom Lane, which he rented in 1840. On his death in 1862, he left an expanded firm to his sons, Frederic, George, Francis and James. Under their control the company diversified to include other household products such as the manufacture of a synthetic ultramarine laundry blue which replaced the

expensive process of grinding lapis lazuli. Products were exported to Canada, and soon overseas businesses were established in Australia, Canada, South Africa and the USA. In 1888, the company was launched on the London Stock Exchange and continued to flourish. In 1890 Zebra Paste grate polish was launched followed in 1899 by the famous Robin brand starch.

The company's famous 'Brasso' was launched in the UK in 1905, and other companies were acquired, including the Master Boot Polish Company and William Berry & Co Ltd.

Jeremiah Colman began in business milling flour and mustard from a watermill near Norwich. When his nephew, James joined him as a partner in 1823, the firm became known as J&J Colman. Soon, larger premises were found in Norwich and the firm diversified into starch, wheat flour and laundry blue. In 1903 J&J Colman

bought Keen, Robinson & Company which produced Keen's mustards, spices, baby foods and Robinson's Patent Barley Water.

Prior to the First World War Reckitt & Sons and J&J Colman were exporting to many of the same markets. Consequently, in 1913, a joint company was established - Atlantis Ltd - in South America. This arrangement was extended in 1921 to cover all trading operations outside the UK.

Also in 1913 Reckitt's went on to join forces with The Chiswick Polish Company (already famed for its Cherry Blossom boot polish and Mansion floor polish), which subsequently merged with the Nugget Polish Company in 1929 to become Chiswick Products Ltd.

A major success occurred in 1933 with the launch of another household name, Dettol.

*Top: Isaac Reckitt (left) and Johann A Benckiser. **Left:** The original mill of 1840. **Above right:** Jeremiah Colman. **Below:** The Dettol filling line in 1935.*

In late 1999 Reckitt & Colman merged with Benckiser, makers of leading brands such as Vanish laundry products and Finish for automatic dishwashers, to form Reckitt Benckiser.

The Benckiser business had been founded in Germany in 1823 by Johann A Benckiser. Until 1956 when Calgon was launched its core business had been exclusively centred on industrial chemicals.

Boots Healthcare International was acquired in 2006 introducing a wide range of well-known selfcare brands including Nurofen, Strepsils and Clearasil.

Today the Reckitt Benckiser Group has operations in 60 countries and sales in 180 countries. It employs more than 23,000 people worldwide.

A holding company was formed in 1938 to manage trading operations in the UK named Reckitt & Colman Ltd. However, the outbreak of the Second World War halted expansion as several factories were damaged by bombs. Despite this, the company made foot powder for the infantry, and Dettol too was used by the troops – though due to the damage to the Dansom Lane site by bombing on the night of 18th July 1941 Dettol production would be switched to Skipton, and would not return to Hull until 1968. After the end of the war Reckitt & Colman launched yet another famous product, Disprin in 1948.

The Group's growth is hardly surprising given the household name status of so many of its products, not just names familiar to our grandparents such as Harpic, Dettol and Disprin, but also far more recent products such as Air Wick, Lemsip, Gaviscon, Woolite and Cillit Bang.

The year 1954 marked the final merging of the separate companies to form Reckitt & Colman Holdings Limited.

Over the following years the company encompassed new markets and evolved into a major international business. The pigment businesses in Europe and Brazil and the Colman's Norwich food business were sold in order to focus on household products and over-the-counter pharmaceuticals. Expansion continued with the acquisition of Airwick Products, Boyle-Midway and L&F Products bringing in further air fresheners, laundry aids and antiseptic brands.

Since the merger of Reckitt & Colman plc and Benckiser in 1999, the Group has experienced remarkable year on year growth and sell an astonishing 15 million products every day.

Top: A birds eye view of the devastation caused to Kingston Works during the bombing of Hull in 1941. ***Above centre:*** *Early products: Robin Starch and Zebra Grate Polish.* ***Right:*** *A selection of products manufactured by Reckitt Benckiser.*

Fenner - Growing Partnerships Worldwide

Administered from its headquarters in Hessle, on the outskirts of Hull, today the Fenner Group employs over 4,000 people worldwide, and has an annual turnover of more than £400 million.

It was in 1861 that Joseph Henry Fenner, a journeyman currier, opened his business in rented premises at Twenty One and a Half Bishop Lane, Hull. Business began with the production of various leather goods, including hosepipes, strap manufacture and leather dressing.

The 1870s saw the firm move more into the production of leather transmission, belting to meet the demand created by rapid industrial growth. The business continued to expand speedily, culminating in the purchase of 18 acres of land in 1890 at Marfleet, then a small village some three miles from the centre of Hull. Plans were drawn up for a new factory and production commenced at Marfleet in 1893.

By the early 1920s the company began to move away from leather towards the production of woven transmission belting. It was that move which laid the foundations for the development of heavyweight conveyor belting for coal mines some 30 years later. Meanwhile endless rubber V-belts had been introduced in the USA. In 1931 an agreement was reached with a USA company for Fenner to market its range of V-belts. The first Fenner-manufactured V-belts left the Marfleet factory in 1937. A year later the company began the production of cast iron pulleys.

In 1937 Fenner became a Public Company with share capital of £250,000.

During the Second World War, in 1941, bombing destroyed the main Marfleet factory; shadow factories in West Yorkshire and Lancashire took over the company's production. Fenner also produced military webbing, parachute harnesses and over 11,000,000 feet of canvas fire hose for the war effort.

Rebuilding of the Marfleet facility began in 1947: in just over a year the first V-belts were produced in the new factory.

During the 1950s manufacturing companies were established in India, Australia and South Africa. The UK also saw significant developments during this period, especially in the area of colliery conveyor belting.

Top left: *Joseph Henry Fenner, founder and sole proprietor from 1861 to 1886.* **Below left:** *Product advertising in 1877.* **Above:** *Electric motor drive.* **Below:** *A view inside an early weaving shed.*

ESTABLISHED 1861.

J. H. FENNER & CO.,
WORKS:—CHAPEL LANE, HULL,
MANUFACTURERS OF
MAIN LEATHER DRIVING BELTS,
DOUBLE AND TREBLE. ANY WIDTH.
SEWN WITH WIRE, LACE, OR HEMP.
SINGLE BELTING.
Endless Thrashing Machine Belts.
DOUBLE AND SINGLE.
Patent Hair Belting.

LEATHER FIRE HOSE.
SEAMLESS WOVEN CANVAS HOSE,
Hydraulic Ram Leathers. Pump Cup Leathers.
INDIA-RUBBER VALVES, WASHERS,
SHEETING, PACKING, &c.
Cotton Waste. Belt Fasteners and Laces of
every description.

Following a colliery disaster in which 80 miners lost their lives when a rubber and canvas conveyor belt was ignited by friction, Fenner launched a programme to develop fire-resistant conveyor belting. The result was Fenaplast, a solid-woven, PVC-impregnated conveyor belting first produced in the Hull factory in 1952 and still in extensive use.

Manufacturing facilities were established in numerous countries, distribution companies acquired, and a Fenner sales and service network developed.

The 1970s saw several acquisitions, including the belt manufacturer James Dawson of Lincoln, and also the company's first major contract for the supply of Fenaplast conveyor belting to China.

In 1984 Fenner purchased the Manheim Belting Company in the USA. Five years later, the BTL business in Leeds was acquired.

During the 1990s major restructuring took place with two rights issues and several acquisitions and disposals. This changed the company from a diverse engineering group into one focussed on reinforced polymer technology.

The power transmission and fluid power businesses were disposed of in 1998 and 2000 respectively. In the same period Fenner acquired the conveyor belting company Scandura in the USA, and also the Conveyor Belting Division (Dunlop) of Unipoly, with facilities in Europe, Australia and the USA.

New conveyor belting manufacturing units were established in China and India whilst the polymer business in the USA was strengthened by the purchase of Efson and Eagle Belting. A significant acquisition took place in 2005 with the purchase of Wellington Holdings, a manufacturer and distributor of specialist oilseals to the energy and mobile equipment industries with bases in UK, USA and Europe. This business was further strengthened by the purchase of EGC based in Houston, Texas, in 2006.

Early in 2008, Fenner acquired Prodesco a USA-based company consisting of two businesses, one manufacturing a range of highly specialised technical fabrics, the second a leader in textile structures for the medical device market.

Later in 2008 the Group acquired Winfield Industries based in Buffalo, USA, a leading supplier of performance critical rollers for digital imaging applications; and King Energy, of New Mexico, USA, specialists in the distribution and servicing of oilfield, gas industry and mining equipment.

Today the Group's activities lie in heavyweight conveyor belting, precision polymer products and advanced sealing technologies with 30 manufacturing facilities worldwide.

Top left: The Marfleet weaving department. Top right: The Hainsworth Research Centre. To keep pace with expansion this purpose built research and development centre housing laboratories, design offices and workshops was opened in Marfleet in 1961, Fenner's centenary year. Centre: A selection of Fenner products: Fenaplast conveyor belt (top), Hallite advanced oil seals (left) and Prodesco specialised technical fabrics and technical structures (right). Below: The Fenner advanced seals and Dawson silicone hose manufacturing facility in Jaiding, China.

Safe with Arco

With its head office in Waverley Street, Hull, and branches throughout Britain, as well as offices in China and India, Arco is the UK's leading supplier of personal protective equipment, workwear and workplace safety products.

The Hull-based, 4th generation family business now has over 110,000 customers and an annual turnover in excess of £220m. Through its team of product specialists, its Big Book product catalogue and a rapidly expanding 39-strong branch network, Arco offers a world-class range of quality assured, branded and own-brand products, carefully selected from ethically compliant suppliers. Products include personal protective equipment, clothing including front and back-of-house career wear, footwear, gloves, workplace safety and hygiene products.

The company is dedicated to its Corporate Social Responsibility policy. In 2005, Arco became a member of the BITC Percent Club by donating 1% of pre-tax profits to charities.

Arco is now also one of Hull's largest employers with over 500 people employed in its Waverley Street Head Office, Hull branch and distinctive 350,000 square foot National Distribution Centre.

The firm was established in 1884 to supply a range of rubber products to industry, although some manufacturing was also undertaken. It is said to have included the production of tennis balls for the then little-known championship at Wimbledon.

The company moved from London to Hull in 1890 because of the shipping trade.

Thomas Martin became Managing Director in 1907, and, after a distinguished career in the Navy, his son, the second Thomas Martin, succeeded him.

The second Thomas Martin began the buyout of the majority of outside shareholders to make Arco a truly family concern.

Things did not always go smoothly. In May 1941 an enemy bomb destroyed all of the company's sales records. It could have signalled the end, but not one customer failed to settle all accounts.

In 1960 Arco moved to new purpose-built premises in Waverley Street, Hull.

The third T Martin (Tom), had joined the firm in 1959, and his brother Stephen in 1964. Together they embarked on a vigorous programme of expansion, establishing branches throughout the country by acquisitions, and by developing on green field sites.

During 1980s the company saw a flurry of expansion, followed in the 1990s by a period of consolidation, though even then growth did not stop.

Tom's son, Thomas, joined the business in 1988.

Stephen Martin's daughter Jo Martin joined the company in 2000.

In 2002 Nicholas Hildyard joined Arco as Finance Director, following a career at Smith and Nephew. At the end of that year Thomas Martin and Jo Martin became Joint MDs. Stephen Martin remained as non-executive Vice-Chairman.

Tom Martin senior retired from the business in 2006, but was appointed as Life President, and remains a non-executive director.

In September 2007 Arco became a member of the Ethical Trading Initiative. The ETI is a high-profile initiative that aims to promote respect for the rights of workers in global supply chains. Other members include M&S, Asda, Boots, WH Smith and Next Retail.

Arco was recognised for its Contribution to the Community achievements at the Mail Publications Awards Ceremony in November 2007, and is awaiting the outcome of the National Business Awards final later this year.

In China, Arco is involved in Project Hope. The company invested in libraries in three schools in Xinjiang, and also fitted out rooms with computer equipment.

In Hull and around its branch network, Arco has been involved in four main projects – The Children's University, Yorkshire Wildlife Trust, Live Music Now! and the Humberside Police Lifestyle Project.

Sadly, on 27th February 2008, Jo Martin, Joint MD, died at the age of only 39. Nicholas Hildyard was subsequently appointed as Joint Managing Director with Thomas Martin. During the previous year Nick had held the role of High Sheriff of the East Riding of Yorkshire, he is also a trustee of Hull Boys Club, The Burton Constable Foundation and Nancie Reckitt Trust.

From its base in Hull in slightly over 100 years Arco has grown from a small jobbing merchant into the country's leading supplier of personal protective equipment, workwear and workplace safety products.

Throughout its history the company, and the family, have been enthusiastic in their support for Hull's community. Tom Martin attributes Arco's success to "determination and the ability to adapt to changing circumstances...we are now carrying the best of our traditional values forward in the 21st century."

*Top, facing page: An early 20th century picture of Arco's shop in Hull. **Bottom, facing page and above:** Exterior and interior views of Arco's National Distribution Centre, Hull. **Below:** Arco's new Portsmouth branch.*

Sparks on the Humber - Humber Electrical

From its headquarters at 45-46 Portland Place in Hull, the Humber Electrical Engineering Company Ltd is involved in all aspects of electrical engineering utilising its wide range of in-house expertise.

Quality and service are of prime importance. The company undertakes full design and build projects involving installation and instrumentation for a large number of customers, including the marine and offshore industries, MoD, public authorities and many large industrial users. Design projects or complete 'Turnkey' projects can be undertaken.

Since before the First World War the company has been designing and installing electrical systems on a variety of vessels ranging from steam driven trawlers and minesweepers up to today's modern chemical and product carriers. Most recently it has designed and installed lightweight systems on fast multi-hulled passenger ferries using gas turbine and waterjet technology.

The company has an unrivalled experience in designing and building magnetic treatment facilities for Naval vessels. It has provided all of the U.K. fixed installations including the facility used by the Vanguard fleet of submarines.

Humber Electrical Engineering was founded by William Ernest Shuttleworth. He was born at Lothersdale in the West Riding and trained at Wolverhampton, arriving in Hull to work at Earles Shipyard as Electrical Manager.

In 1908 William left Earles to form his own electrical company. Now it is hard to recall just how cutting edge electrical work then was. The modern electric light bulb was only a little over 25 years old. Just ten years before William Shuttleworth set up on his own Marconi had been demonstrating the remarkable power of radio to transmit a message over a distance of just three miles.

In 1911 the firm moved to Portland Place where the company still has its headquarters. From the beginning the firm specialised in complete electrical installations on ships and was a pioneer in the fitting of electric light on trawlers.

WE Shuttleworth patented and manufactured several trawler light fittings which were still in use until quite

Above: Founder, WE Shuttleworth. Left: One of the merchant ships fitted with electric light by the company. Below: An early advertisement for the Humber Electrical Engineering Company.

THE HUMBER ELECTRICAL
ENGINEERING Co.,
45 & 46, PORTLAND PLACE, HULL

Electrical Engineers & Contractors.

Complete Installation:
Works, Country Houses, Ships, &c.
REPAIRS & ACCESSORIES.

Nat. Tel. 958.   Telegrams "Humber Electric"

recently. Small DC generating sets were also designed and manufactured, and in one year alone over fifty ships at Swansea had his sets installed. Teams of men worked at shipyards all over the country. As a result of many enquiries, the Company undertook its first land installations in 1926, when many farms and country estates received electricity for the first time.

The New Theatre in Hull was one of their prestigious jobs prior to the Second World War. During the war the Company's entire resources were geared to the war effort, including the complete electrical installation on coastal minesweepers, corvettes and a large number of merchant ships. Altogether work was completed on over 160 new vessels.

Today, after investing heavily in computerised equipment, the Company is working throughout the UK, the rest of Europe, Japan and South America. It is involved in all aspects of electrical engineering for marine and offshore industries, the MoD, public authorities and many large industries.

Some recent prestigious projects include the electrical design and equipment package for Offshore Patrol Vessels - VT Shipbuilders; the manufacture of an integrated bridge system for QM2 - Chantiers de L'Atlantique, the main switchboard for FPSO conversion FSU Soorena – Singapore and complete electrical design and installation on several luxury yachts for DML, design and supply of switchgear for offshore wave power generation projects, design and manufacture of new cargo handling switchgear for Shell Liquid Gas Carriers, magnetic treatment facility for MOD submarines at the Faslane base and a special fountain display project for the King of Bahrain.

In the immediate post-war years Humber Electrical was closely involved in the rebuilding of many well known local landmarks, including Hammonds, Willis Ludlow, the Co-op and Drypool Bridge. Originally all electrical equipment had to be manufactured and designed in-house because it was not possible to pop down to the local wholesalers and buy equipment off the shelf as it is today. Switchboards would be manufactured with an open front and have knife switches mounted on slate or a type of fibreboard. By contrast switchboards today are what is called 'dead front' which means that all the electrical parts are fully insulated and shrouded from accidental damage.

Mr SN Shuttleworth, the only son of Mr WE Shuttleworth joined the company in 1933, followed by his son Mr CE Shuttleworth who joined the company in 1975. CE Shuttleworth was Managing Director until his death in 2007. Now his sister Ms EM Shuttleworth is Managing Director of the company founded by her grandfather so long ago.

This page: Recent projects for Humber Electricals: Offshore patrol vessels (top right) FSU Soorena - Singapore (above left) and is QM2 - Chantiers de L'Atlantique (below).

Acknowledgments

The publishers would like to pay special and sincere thanks to the following individuals and organisations for their help and contribution to make this publication possible

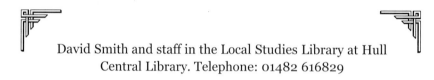

David Smith and staff in the Local Studies Library at Hull
Central Library. Telephone: 01482 616829

Staff in the library and imaging departments at the Hull Daily Mail
www.thisishull.co.uk

National Monuments Record (NMR), the public archive of
English Heritage.
For further information about these images please telephone
01793 414600 or email nmrinfo@english-heritage.org.uk

Harry Cartlidge with kind permission from Arthur Credland,
Curator of the Hull Maritime Museum.
www.hull.gov.uk - Telephone: 01482 613902

A number of photographs within this publication were taken
by the late Donald Innes (1908-1971). The publishers would
therefore like to thank David Innes, Stephen Betts and the
staff at Innes for their valuable help and contribution.
Innes Photographers,11-13 The Square Hessle, HU13 0AF.
Telephone: 01482 649271 - www.innes.co.uk